The Critical Idiom

Founder Editor: JOHN D. JUMP (1969–1976)

9 Realism

Realism/*Damian Grant*

Methuen & Co Ltd

First published 1970
by Methuen & Co Ltd
11 New Fetter Lane, London EC4P 4EE
Reprinted 1974 and 1978

© 1970 Damian Grant

Printed in Great Britain
by J. W. Arrowsmith Ltd, Bristol

ISBN 0 416 17820 0

Distributed in the U.S.A. by
HARPER & ROW PUBLISHERS, INC.
BARNES & NOBLE IMPORT DIVISION

For TERESA: *sine qua non*

Contents

General Editor's Preface

This volume is one of a series of short studies, each dealing with a single key item, or a group of two or three key items, in our critical vocabulary. The purpose of the series differs from that served by the standard glossaries of literary terms. Many terms are adequately defined for the needs of students by the brief entries in these glossaries, and such terms will not be the subjects of studies in the present series. But there are other terms which cannot be made familiar by means of compact definitions. Students need to grow accustomed to them through simple and straightforward but reasonably full discussions of them. The purpose of this series is to provide such discussions.

Some of the terms in question refer to literary movements (e.g., 'Romanticism', 'Aestheticism', etc.), others to literary kinds (e.g., 'Comedy', 'Epic', etc.), and still others to stylistic features (e.g., 'Irony', 'The Conceit', etc.). Because of this diversity of subject-matter, no attempt has been made to impose a uniform pattern upon the studies. But all authors have tried to provide as full illustrative quotation as possible, to make reference whenever appropriate to more than one literature, and to compose their studies in such a way as to guide readers towards the short bibliographies in which they have made suggestions for further reading.

John D. Jump

University of Manchester

Acknowledgements

I should like to thank Professor Jump for the interest he has taken in this study, and his attentive criticism made early and late in the composition; also Dr Lilian Furst, for her conversation on the subject and the loan of some useful books; and especially the willing help given by my wife Teresa, who restrained my translations whilst typing the text (as she alone is able to) from my unmannerly handwriting.

NOTE AND ABBREVIATIONS

In order to avoid redundancy, I have not in every instance given both the original and a translation of material quoted from the French. Where it seemed easily understandable I have sometimes left only the French; often I have simply given an English translation, with a reference to the French source.

For ease of reference to a small number of books (full details of which may be found in the bibliography) I have used the following abbreviations:

AN	Henry James *The Art of the Novel*
DMLR	George J. Becker *Documents of Modern Literary Realism*
ECN	Kenneth Graham *English Criticism of the Novel 1865–1900*
GH	Harry Levin *The Gates of Horn*
OP	Wallace Stevens *Opus Posthumous*
RE	Émile Zola *Le Roman Expérimental*
RN	J. H. Bornecque et P. Cogny *Réalisme et Naturalisme*
RNS	Roland S. Stromberg *Realism, Naturalism, Symbolism*

'Realism is a corruption of reality'

WALLACE STEVENS

I

Introduction

If, as Henry James claimed, 'the Novel remains still, under the right persuasion, the most independent, most elastic, most prodigious of literary forms' (*AN*, p. 326) then the word realism – so often invoked in the discussion of it – must surely be the most independent, most elastic, most prodigious of critical terms. But whereas the qualities James celebrates extend the possibilities of a literary form, they are more likely to restrict the possibilities of a critical term; and certainly the word realism, with its apparent independence of any formal, contentual, or qualitative description, and its unmanageable elasticity, is a prodigy that most people feel they could do well without.

Nothing illustrates the chronic instability of the word more clearly than its uncontrollable tendency to attract another qualifying word, or words, to provide some kind of semantic support. The curious reader will not have to adventure far into critical literature before coming upon some of the following, which I have arranged in alphabetical order since they could not be persuaded to obey any other: critical realism, durational realism, dynamic realism, external realism, fantastic realism, formal realism, ideal realism, infra-realism, ironic realism, militant realism, naïve realism, national realism, naturalist realism, objective realism, optimistic realism, pessimistic realism, plastic realism, poetic realism, psychological realism, quotidian realism, romantic realism, satiric realism, socialist realism, subjective realism, super-subjective realism, visionary realism. Many of these will be found scattered in George J. Becker's collection of documents on realism; others are from modern criticism. Wimsatt and Brooks create a scale of low realism, high realism, and drab realism in their *Literary Criticism* (p. 102); Walter Lacher's book *Le Réalisme dans le roman contemporain* is a successive categorizing of different realisms, Chateaubriand's 'réalisme pastoral', Duhamel's 'réalisme spiritualiste', Proust's 'réalisme du moi profond', and even Jules Romains' 'réalisme de la plus grande ville' (pp. 332–3).

One can sympathize therefore with Becker's mild suggestion that 'it would add to ease of discourse in the future if whatever happens next should be given a new name and not be tagged by some variant or permutation of the word "realism" ' (*DMLR*, p. 37). Also with the practising critic who reminds us that ' "realism" is a notoriously treacherous concept' (Mark Kinkead-Weekes and Ian Gregor, *William Golding:* a *Critical Study*, London, 1967, p. 121); who says – perhaps with some impatience – 'I do not want to get bogged down in definitions of the word *realism*' (W. J. Harvey, *The Art of George Eliot*, London, 1961, pp. 50–1) and simply gets on with the word as well as he can, leaving it to generate a meaning in the critical context itself; or who declares – of Harold Pinter – that 'all question of realism or fantasy, naturalism or artifice becomes irrelevant, and indeed completely meaningless' (John Russell Taylor, *Anger and After*; 2nd ed., London, 1969, p. 358). Roland Stromberg authorizes this scepticism of theory when he says that 'realism and naturalism must be defined by their historical content. The terms were short-hand for certain cultural phenomena of the times, and can be grasped only through a study of these phenomena' (*RNS*, p. xix).

The word is in fact delinquent, and writers have indicated their mistrust of its behaviour either by sending it out under escort (as in the above list) or by letting it loose only when safely hand-cuffed by inverted commas. Ortega y Gasset makes it quite clear that he adopts the latter course on principle: 'I cannot now discuss this involved term which I have been careful always to use in quotation marks to render it suspect' (*The Dehumanization of Art*, p. 102).

II

If one wishes to achieve a genuine discrimination between the unruly meanings of realism as they jostle and overlap then one must accept the necessity of going back to the philosophers. René Wellek deliberately avoids what he sees as 'the whole fundamental epistemological problem . . . of the relation of art to reality' in his chapter on realism in *Concepts of Criticism* (p. 224), and the temptation is to provide (as he does) an historical account. As we have seen, Roland Stromberg considers this the only one possible. But the drawback here is that one achieves no critical view of the word's uses, and no sense emerges as preferable to (or even properly distinguishable from) another; one needs some basic orientations, however simple, in order to structure this semantic flux.

Realism is a critical term only by adoption from philosophy: it comes weakened from loss of blood in earlier battles, and one needs at least to be able to distinguish the opposing sides before one can decide which state is being challenged, and which advanced. Nor is this easy, because 'realism' has been distracted by the service of different philosophical masters, and has no exclusive or unqualified loyalty to any of them. Although the company it kept during the middle of the nineteenth century – at the time of its going into general circulation – was aggressively materialist, leaving ineradicable traces on its present character, it originally served idealism, and was used to describe the scholastic doctrine that universals (justice, goodness, etc.) have a real existence, independent of the particular objects in which they are found. This was maintained in opposition to conceptualism (which held that universals existed only in the mind) and nominalism (which denied the existence of universals altogether: they were simply names). Even at this stage there were qualifications: 'extreme realism' and 'mitigated realism' indicated variations of emphasis in the idea.

It was in the eighteenth century with Thomas Reid's 'common-sense school' that realism assumed in philosophy the sharply different sense which was to have such a fatal – or at least confusing – attraction for writers, critics, and theorists in literature. Here it proclaimed that the objects of perception *are* objects, and have a real existence outside the perceiving mind; which idea was developed in opposition to all forms of idealism. Following 'the Scottish tradition of "natural realism" ', and resisting what John Passmore describes as the main tendency of nineteenth-century thought 'towards the conclusion that both "things" and facts about things are dependent for their existence and their nature upon the operations of a mind' (*A Hundred Years of Philosophy*, Pelican ed., Harmondsworth, 1968, pp. 279, 174), naïve realists, new realists, and critical realists all claimed the word to designate – with progressive subtlety – the idea of an external, physical existence independent of mind.

With its loyalties divided (however unequally) between idealism and materialism it may seem that realism has forgotten its duty to reality itself. And the reason is that the concept of reality, too, has exploded in the modern mind: this brings us to the source of our difficulties. Philip Rahv observes that it is no longer possible to use realistic methods 'without taking reality for granted' – and this is precisely what artists cannot now do: 'it is reality itself which they bring into question' (*DMLR*, p. 589). Wordsworth was prepared, at least in theory, to take reality for granted, as is evident from the kind of criteria he used in his preface to the *Lyrical Ballads*; but it is significant that Coleridge, made cautious by metaphysics, rejected Wordsworth's terms, and accused him particularly of 'an equivocation in the use of the word "real" ' ' (*Biographia Literaria*, ch. 17). It will seem to us today impossible to avoid the charge of equivocation in using the noun 'reality' or the adjective 'real' at all. Vladimir Nabokov, indeed, exercises the same caution with 'reality' as Ortega does with 'realism': he says in his postcript to *Lolita* that it is 'one of the few words which can mean nothing without quotes' (Corgi ed., London, 1967, p. 329). Bernard Bergonzi argues in a recent symposium that we are unable to write now as Tolstoy did 'because we have no common sense of reality. We are saddled with all kinds of relativistic structures of consciousness. We do not believe in there being one reality "out there" as undoubtedly Tolstoy did' ('Realism, Reality, and the Novel', a Symposium reported by Park Honan, *Novel* II (1969) p. 200).

Philosophers, then, will disdain such treacherous footing. It is generally recognized that philosophy today has given up all pretension to what was once thought of as its first function – providing knowledge of reality – and is content to concentrate its energy on a collateral function, that of investigating the possibility of knowledge at all. Philosophy shrinks to epistemology. 'As to what reality is, I take no great interest' said the new realist E. B. Holt (Passmore, *op. cit.*, p. 263). And so the concept of reality finds itself abandoned like some useless fortification, where poets, novelists, and other less responsible writers may play soldiers if they wish.

Which of course they do: more convincingly than the philosopher may be happy to acknowledge. For it is widely held, again, that it is creative writers rather than professional philosophers who have done most of the philosophical thinking during the twentieth century; of that kind, at least, which 'returns to men's business and bosoms'. Modern writers conduct as if by instinct a systematic critique of reality: 'it is reality itself which they bring into question' with an imaginativeness and sense of relevance that the philosopher has (apparently) forfeited. Reality is seen as something which has to be attained, not merely taken for granted; and the attainment is a continuous process that never allows the concept to stabilize, or the word to offer a convenient mould of meaning.

Having said this, one recognizes that some writers will nevertheless be working towards some kind of stability in the idea, whilst others will be working away from it. The examples of Eliot, Joyce, and Lawrence will serve as an illustration of differing intentions in the presentation of reality. Eliot was committed to a Christian belief by the time he came to write his plays, and this is no doubt why we may observe a centripetal tendency in his characters' discovery of reality. Becket's whole endeavour in *Murder in the Cathedral* is towards an understanding of his own actions, a purification of motive worked by undeluded self-knowledge; an effort to contradict the Tempters' cynicism:

> All things become less real, man passes
> From unreality to unreality.

Becket realizes, in a line repeated in *Four Quartets*, that 'Human kind cannot bear very much reality'; it is his determination to face this himself, and bring others to face it (*Collected Plays*, London, 1962, pp. 28, 43). At the beginning of *The Cocktail Party* Edward Chamberlayne is faced with the fact that his wife has left him; he is made aware of his 'obsolete responses', realizes that he 'must find out who she is, to find out who I am', and having had 'the unreality /Of the role she had always imposed upon me' revealed to him, he can at last set about the process of readjustment (pp. 136, 176). In the same play Peter Quilpe speaks of his encounter with Celia as 'My first experience of reality', and Celia herself declares she has at last been made aware by what has happened of the reality of her situation (pp. 143, 186). The start of *The Family Reunion* shows Harry Monchensey reacting against his family's protective behaviour, and although he fears reality – 'the most real is what I fear' – still insists on pursuing it beyond their limited perspectives: 'What you call the normal/Is merely the unreal and the unimportant'; his own horrified guilt is 'too real for your words to alter' (pp. 90, 98, 99). But the difficulty of establishing 'a reality' is evident from his later words to Agatha, 'what did not happen is as true as what did happen' (p. 107): however common the endeavour, however much it seeks the centre, it is after all only the centre of the self that is being sought.

The inevitably subjective and therefore indeterminate status of reality is powerfully dramatized in Joyce's *A Portrait of the Artist as a Young Man*, in which Joyce follows Stephen Dedalus's developing consciousness of different levels of reality, from the simple sensuous reality of a child's sensations to the liberated reality of the disengaged imagination. The novel describes a continuous process of dilation, as Stephen is 'drawn to go forth to encounter reality'; there is always some further realization at hand that will conduct him to that core of consciousness which is (for him) the ground of the real. Stephen explicitly states he will 'fly by those nets' personal, religious, and national, which would limit his exploration of reality; 'I go to encounter for the millionth time the reality of experience and to forge in the smithy of my soul the uncreated conscience of my race' (Penguin ed., Harmondsworth, 1968, pp. 159, 203, 253). And we reach the logical conclusion of this distribution of reality in Lawrence, where the word reaches its most fluid condition as it is used crucially but quite capriciously to qualify the shifting states of his characters' consciousness. This is particularly evident in Lawrence's presentation of Ursula Brangwen in *The Rainbow* (and later in *Women in Love*). Reality for Ursula exists in her own stimulated consciousness. So when she is obsessed by thoughts of her future career as a teacher, her father sitting at the table becomes less real than her fancies (Penguin ed., Harmondsworth, 1968, p. 362). The schoolroom in Ilkeston proves to be a 'hard, raw reality', a 'limited reality', but its very unpleasantness, its 'stark reality', makes it more real, in that it occasions more of a reaction in her, than for example her home, which recedes to a 'minor reality' (pp. 367, 373). Her sexual experience with Skrebensky later in the book introduces her to a new level of reality, which again takes precedence over others: 'they themselves were reality, all outside was tribute to them... They alone inhabited the world of reality. All the rest lived on a lower sphere' (pp. 454–5). But even this is not then an 'established' reality: she can still cancel it by withdrawing her imaginative assent. Reality is 'ever-changing' with her; and when she does soon reject Skrebensky, she decides that he 'had never become finally real' to her, 'she had created him for the time being' (pp. 456, 494).

According to this usage, reality is not only located in the mind, but is at the mercy of the moods and caprices of that mind, dilates and contracts with the degree of activity of the consciousness. Reality is 'for the time being'. The concept of reality is utterly atomized by this extreme subjectivity of viewpoint, and such usage as Lawrence's (which is extreme but not untypical) seriously prejudices the word's retention in more analytical contexts. Here, obviously, is no path for the philosopher or theorist to follow. Reality runs before the mind:

> Reality is like a float that rides
> all efforts of the irritated mind
> to frame its definition: or a fish,
> that swallows up all other forms of life
> and then drinks off the sea in which it swims.

The analytical thinker must be content to follow, with no thought of overtaking it, on the slower steps of truth.

III

To Pilate's question 'What is Truth?' philosophy gives not just different answers but different kinds of answer, representing different approaches to the question; and it is possible to divide these approaches – in all their 'skeined stained veined variety' – into two groups which are contrasting, complementary; 'part, pen, pack' the plotters of truth into Hopkins's 'two flocks, two folds'. Truth may accordingly be seen as either scientific or poetic; discovered by a process of knowing or created by a process of making. The first is technically referred to as the correspondence theory, and the second as the coherence theory.

The correspondence theory is empirical and epistemological. It involves a naïve or common-sense realist belief in the reality of the external world (as expressed in Dr Johnson's kicking a stone to prove that matter exists) and supposes that we may come to know this world by observation and comparison. The truth it proposes is the truth that corresponds, approximates to the predicated reality, *renders* it with fidelity and accuracy; the truth of the positivist, the determinist, whose aim is to document, delimit, and define. 'You defer to the fact,' says Becket to his persecutors in *Murder in the Cathedral*; the correspondence theory defers automatically to the fact, and requires that truth be verified by reference to it. It is democratic; it takes its confidence from the substantial agreement of the majority in its description of reality, which it therefore calls objective.

In the coherence theory, on the other hand, the epistemological process is accelerated or elided by intuitive perception. Truth is not earned by the labour of documentation and analysis but coined, a ready synthesis, and made current – as is any currency – by confidence, 'the confidence of truth'. Evidence is replaced by self-evidence.

In the first case the truth is true *to* something, in the second it is true as a line or edge is said to be true when it is straight, flawless – *containing* the truth, not simply representing or alluding to it. In the first case reality is as it were waylaid by truth, arrested by it; in the second reality is discovered and in a sense created in the very act of perception. The one is a capture, the other a release.

To illustrate the difference, one might say that the truth of Donne's apostrophe to the sun

> Shine here to us, and thou art every where;
> This bed thy center is, these walls, thy sphere

does not depend on the scientific truth of the ptolemaic cosmology. (Donne could write, where it suited him,

> The Sun is lost, and th'earth, and no mans wit
> Can well direct him where to looke for it).

'The Sunne Rising' develops an imaginative idea, an hypothesis, which is made plausible by the fact that it is made at all.

Bertrand Russell suggests that the correspondence theory is a *semantic*, and the coherence theory a *syntactic* conception of truth; one probes for and refers to a verifiable meaning, the other makes a true statement – like a dam in the mind – in the space behind which reality accumulates. Conceptions of language are indeed central to the whole question. Locke in his *Essay Concerning Human Understanding* (1690) elaborated a theory of language which related it to sense-impressions, bound it mechanically to the physical world:

> It may also lead us a little toward the original of all our notions of knowledge, if we remark how great a dependence our words have on common sensible ideas ... and I doubt not but, if we could trace them to their sources, we should find, in all languages, the names which stand for things that fall not under our senses to have had their first rise from sensible ideas.
>
> (Bk. III, Ch. 1, sec. 5)

This simplistic account largely satisfied the eighteenth century, where words were complacently thought of as 'the images of things', and Locke's thesis may be seen as the source of all empirical theory of language. This whole approach – which still has its apologists – is exposed by a relentless process of *reductio ad absurdum* in Samuel Beckett's second novel, *Watt*, where the central character (whose 'imagination had never been a lively one') seeks naïvely to trap the world in words, define it, understand it, then put it away: 'to explain had always been to exorcize, for Watt'. His whole activity is a 'wrapping up safe in words', he needs to make 'a pillow of old words, for his head'. But gradually the world recedes from his verbal grasp: 'Watt now found himself in the midst of things which, if they consented to be named, did so as it were with reluctance'; he panics; his 'need of semantic succour was at times so great that he would set to trying names on things, and on himself, almost as a woman hats'; and eventually degenerates into complete incoherence as language falls back from its arrogant attempt on the impossible (Calder & Boyars, London, 1963, pp. 74–82, 162–7). Compare the 'profound epistemological experience' which Tony Tanner sees in *Moby Dick*: Melville 'gathers together every possible definition and description of a whale that's ever been, and what he shows is that you can never catch a live whale. You can only have a dead whale' ('Realism, Reality, and the Novel', *Novel*, II (1969), p. 206).

A more sophisticated theory sees language not simply as an image of reality but as an instrument in terms of which reality is realized – made real; carrying within its own declarative structure the material of truth, so that there can be no appeal made outside the inclusive conventions of this system to the dumb materiality of the world of things. Truth and falsehood become properties of language alone, to which 'reality' – that impossible hypothesis – is both indifferent and irrelevant. As Ernst Cassirer says, 'in the struggle between metaphysics and language, language has come off victorious ... the sensationalist view of the world has gradually changed into a purely symbolic view' (*The Philosophy of Symbolic Forms*, New Haven 1953, n.e. 1966, vol. 1, Language; p. 139).

The development between Wittgenstein's early and late theories of language might be seen as a progression from a semantic (correspondence) theory in the *Tractatus Logico-Philosophicus* to a syntactical (coherence) theory in his *Philosophical Investigations*. 'In the *Tractatus*' said Wittgenstein in 1932, 'I was unclear about "logical analysis" and the clarification it suggests. At that time I thought it provided a "connexion between language and Reality".' Later, the 'crucial problem now became, "By what procedures do men *establish* links between language and the real world?" ' (cit. Stephen Toulmin, 'Ludwig Wittgenstein', *Encounter*, Jan. 1969, pp. 62, 67). It is the fact that these links have to be *established* (by what Toulmin calls 'behavioural semantics') that approximates Wittgenstein's later position to the coherence theory.

Neither view of truth, neither view of language, may be maintained in total contradiction of or even independence of the other. As so often, it is ultimately a matter of emphasis: Wittgenstein does not contradict but merely qualifies his earlier ideas importantly. Beckett never settles into simple solipsism, or a finally subjective view of language: the voice in *The Unnamable* sees himself 'made of words', but they are 'others' words' as well as his own; 'inside me, outside me' (in *Molloy, Malone Dies and The Unnamable*, Calder & Boyars, London, 1966, p. 390). It was suggested long ago by Wilhelm von Humboldt that language is precisely that unique nexus which links the subjective with the objective world; Ernst Cassirer gives an illuminating account of Humboldt's theories in his own volume on language (pp. 91–3, 155–62).

This idea of an interpenetration between the world and the consciousness, body and mind, is one whose full implications are still being explored: the equation between the two spheres is infinitely subtle, perhaps inexpressible, and now seems, and now seems not, to exist. Merleau-Ponty saw language as 'a perfect illustration of the dialectical relationship between ourselves and the world', and coerced it into a central position in his phenomenology; for him, man 'neither merely makes nor merely encounters the world he lives in' (Passmore, *op. cit.*, p. 502).

But despite the attempt at reconciliation that is perpetually being made between these two orders, as they focus on the medium (language) or the object (truth), and although one ought to suspect any crude contrast drawn between them, the difference of emphasis is marked and wholly warrants the distinction I have made above between 'correspondence' and 'coherence'. This distinction I shall now invoke to discriminate at a fundamental level between the divergent meanings of realism in literature.

IV

In all the uses of realism one can discern a similar tension between correspondence and coherence as the criterion of reality reflected or achieved.

The correspondence theory of realism is the expression of what one might call the conscience of literature: the conscience which protests when it neglects or disparages external reality, and seeks to draw its sustenance from, and exist for, the disengaged imagination alone – as Dr Johnson called it, that 'vagrant and licentious faculty'. It is the conscience which prompted Rimbaud's recantation at the end of *Une Saison en Enfer*: '. . . je dois enterrer mon imagination et mes souvenirs . . . moi qui me suis dit mage ou ange, dispensé de toute morale, je suis rendu au sol, avec un devoir à chercher, et la réalité rugueuse à étreindre . . . je demanderai pardon pour m'être nourri de mensonge' [I must bury my imagination and my memories . . . I who called myself magus or angel, absolved from all morality, I am given back to the earth, with a task to pursue, and wrinkled reality to embrace . . . I shall ask forgiveness for having fed on lies] (*Rimbaud*, Penguin ed., Harmondsworth, 1962, p. 345); the conscience which made Yeats exclaim, in the last lines of his late poem 'The Circus Animals' Desertion':

> I must lie down where all the ladders start,
> In the foul rag-and-bone shop of the heart

-- the conscience which is active in the poetry and poetic of Wallace Stevens, and which may be summarized by a dictum from his 'Adagia': 'Eventually an imaginary world is entirely without interest' (*OP*, p. 175).

It is in the spirit of this realism that literature seeks to deliver itself up to the real world, to open its gates submissively to the horses of instruction; to ballast its giddy imagination with the weight of truth, and submit its forms, conventions, and consecrated attitudes to the purifying ravishment of fact. This realism is the 'appeal open from criticism to nature' which Johnson allows in his *Preface to Shakespeare*, although it is now the falsifications of literature not criticism that are appealed against; this realism seeks to eliminate that special category or artistic convention which Johnson declared was 'received as true even by those who in daily experience feel it to be false'.

Realism as the conscience of literature confesses that it owes a duty, some kind of reparation, to the real world – a real world to which it submits itself unquestioningly. George J. Becker is clearly writing of this conscience when he says in his Introduction 'whatever reality is, it seems safe to say that it is not identical with a work of art and is anterior to it. Realism, then, is a formula of art which, conceiving of reality in a certain way, undertakes to present a simulacrum of it . . . ' (*DMLR*, p. 36). And in his own selection of documents he clearly favours this view – which is, of course, that most generally accepted. Thus the early Russian critic Belinsky argues for a 'poetry of reality' which 'does not create life anew, but reproduces it'; the materialist Chernishevsky maintains 'the first purpose of art is to reproduce reality'; William Dean Howells chastises 'the foolish old superstition that literature and art are anything but the expression of life, and are to be judged by any other test than of their fidelity to it' (pp. 41–2, 64, 133).

As conscience is vitiated and confused with scruples, so this conception of realism degenerates into literalism – a representational literalism that finds its final expression in the classroom aesthetics of Mr Bounderby in the second chapter of *Hard Times*.

'You must discard the word Fancy altogether. You have nothing to do with it. You are not to have, in any object of use or ornament, what would be a contradiction in fact. You don't walk upon flowers in fact; you cannot be allowed to walk upon flowers in carpets. You don't find that foreign birds and butterflies come and perch upon your crockery; you cannot be permitted to paint foreign birds and butterflies upon your crockery. You never meet with quadrupeds going up and down walls; you must not have quadrupeds represented upon walls. You must use,' said the gentleman, 'for all these purposes, combinations and modifications (in primary colours) of mathematical figures which are susceptible of proof and demonstration. This is the new discovery. This is fact. This is taste.'

It is the troubled conscience of realism that accords a special value to such things today as the documentary drama, the 'novel of fact', and confessional poetry;[1] a value which is applied illegitimately from without instead of being generated within the work, and is awarded to pretension rather than performance.

The coherence theory of realism, on the other hand, is the consciousness of literature: its self-awareness, its realization of its own ontological status. Here realism is achieved not by imitation, but by creation; a creation which, working with the materials of life, absolves these by the intercession of the imagination from mere factuality and translates them to a higher order. Henry James referred to this process as a 'sacrament of execution', and describes how an element declining this translation, persisting as 'the impression not artistically dealt with', 'shames the honour offered it and can only be spoken of as having ceased to be a thing of fact and yet not become a thing of truth' (*AN*, pp. 115–16, 230–1). Fact and truth: the two are proposed by James here as alternative not synonymous, and it is the liberation from a facile identification of

---

[1] See my concluding Note.

the two that brings realism to its majority in consciousness. For the conscious realist reality is *not* 'anterior': 'Reality in the artist's sense is always something created; it does not exist *a priori*' (A. A. Mendilow, *Time and the Novel*, London, 1952, p. 36); and therefore he owes no menial service to it: there is nothing to correspond *to*. Benedetto Croce stated unequivocally that 'there is no nature or reality outside the mind and the artist need not worry about the relationship' (cit. Wellek, *Concepts of Criticism*, p. 238). J. W. Purser maintains the same position more soberly in an article 'The Artistic Approach to Truth': 'If ... there is any truth in a work of art it is not generally found to be in its correspondence with or imitation of actual fact' (*British Journal of Aesthetics*, III (1963), p. 99). 'The Circus Animals' Desertion' – Yeats's concentrated poetic autobiography – again offers an image of this realism, asserting its unilateral reality outside any idea of correspondence:

> Heart-mysteries there, and yet when all is said
> It was the dream itself enchanted me:
> Character isolated by a deed
> To engross the present and dominate memory.
> Players and painted stage took all my love,
> And not those things that they were emblems of.

Here is where conscience supervenes to remind Yeats of where these images began – 'In the foul rag-and-bone shop of the heart' – but the mood of imaginative independence is not to be dismissed; in his moments of greatest confidence it will always seem to the artist his lawful ambition. So it seemed to Blake when he wrote in *Jerusalem*:

> I must Create a System or be enslav'd by another Man's.
> I will not Reason & Compare: my business is to Create.

So it seemed to Flaubert when, fatigued by the novelist's eternal labour of rendering, he wrote in his celebrated letter to Louise Colet of 1852:

Ce qui me semble beau, ce que je voudrais faire, c'est un livre sur rien, un livre sans attache extérieure, qui se tiendrait de lui-même par la force interne de son style, comme la terre sans être soutenue se tient en l'air, un livre qui n'aurait presque pas de sujet ou du moins où le sujet serait presque invisible, si cela se peut . . .

[What seems to me ideal, what I should like to do, is to write a book about nothing, a book with no reference to anything outside itself, which would stand on its own by the inner strength of its style, just as the earth holds itself without support in space, a book which would have almost no subject or at least where the subject should be almost imperceptible, if that were possible.]

(*Correspondance*, II 345–6)

There could be no clearer, more final statement of the coherence theory of realism than this – and no plainer illustration of how this theory supersedes the clumsier idea of establishing truth by the laborious process of correspondence. The novel Flaubert envisages is absolved from 'attache extérieure', disdains such an ignominious appeal to reality, and relies instead on 'la force interne de son style': style seen here as a conviction that gathers among the words, that style which Flaubert describes later in the same letter as 'une manière absolue de voir les choses'; that is a way of *creating*, since any reference to the 'absolute' involves an idealist metaphysic.

But this is, as Flaubert himself recognized ('si cela se peut'), the statement of an ideal, and an unrealizable ideal. The hypothesis is exciting and instructive, but a book cannot be written about nothing;

> For, nor in nothing, nor in things
> Extreme, and scatt'ring bright, can love inhere . . .

as Donne wrote in his poem 'Aire and Angels'; the consciousness cannot escape from the body altogether, dispense altogether with the 'ballast' of its material conditions. What Cassirer has to say about the linguistic theories of idealism is directly relevant to Flaubert's chimerical ambition: 'language and word strive for the expression of pure being; but they never attain to it, because in them the designation of something other, of an accidental 'attribute' of the object, is mixed with the designation of this pure being' (*op. cit.*, p. 126). The novelist – the poet also – must involve himself with the accidental, the material, even if he does not submit to it.

'The inter-relation between reality and imagination is the basis of the character of literature' (*OP*, p. 294); this is the theme which Wallace Stevens takes up again and again in his own subtle adjustments of the perennial equation. 'Reality is not what it is. It consists of the many realities which it can be made into' – 'no fact is a bare fact', neither is any individual 'a universe in itself' – 'the interaction between things is what makes them fecund' (pp. 178, 237). It is in this spirit that he rejects surrealism: 'the essential fault of surrealism is that it invents without discovering', and maintains that 'eventually an imaginary world is entirely without interest' (pp. 177, 175). For: 'In poetry at least the imagination must not detach itself from reality' (p. 161). He describes poetry cryptically as 'sticking to the facts in a world in which there are no facts', and resorts to an even more deliberate paradox: 'Literature is the better part of life. To this it seems inevitably necessary to add, provided life is the better part of literature' (pp. 254, 158). But paradox is more profitable than polemic, and Stevens is all the time pursuing his idea of the intimate relation and mutual validation of subject and object. *Esse est percipi*: to be is to be perceived; *esse est percipere*: to be is to perceive; Berkeley's complementary theses are endlessly echoed in Stevens's work. And the reward for this maintained tension is the occasional attainment of their unity:

> Perhaps there is a degree of perception at which what is real and what is imagined are one: a state of clairvoyant observation, accessible or possibly accessible to the poet or, say, the acutest poet. (p. 166)

V

And so realism – 'that effort, that willed tendency of art to approx-
imate reality' (Harry Levin, *GH*, p. 3) – is not one tendency but
two, the possible ultimate reconciliation of which should not
obscure their practical contrariety. This opposition has in fact
been only too luridly dramatized by literary polemic, the general
shallowness of which is clearly exposed when the full context of the
contrasts is understood. Thus it is not simply a matter of some
novels being 'false' and others 'true', as Edmond and Jules de
Goncourt blandly assert in their preface to *Germinie Lacerteux*
(1865); one obviously has to qualify this with the realization that
different novelists may subscribe to different criteria of truth.

For the two chapters that follow I shall take up with appropriate
caution the distinction I have outlined (and whose outlines I have
softened) to study the emergence of the idea of realism in nineteenth-century France, where it received a local habitation and a
name, and its gradual qualification in the wider republic of letters.

2

Conscientious Realism

I

The conscience that awoke to find itself called realism was stirred from the dreams of the romantics by a group of artists in mid-nineteenth-century France. But these writers and painters were unwilling to see this movement of mind as a 'movement' in the traditional sense, and were even more unwilling to define or delimit it in any way other than negatively. So the word 'réalisme' – 'mot drapeau', 'mot bête' as Edmond de Goncourt called it in the preface to *Les Frères Zemganno* – was accepted only after due demonstration of reluctance by these artists as a provocative and provisional 'étiquette' or label, an inadequate and necessarily equivocal focus for their diverse activities. The painter Courbet set the words 'Du Réalisme' over the door of the exhibition of his rejected paintings in 1855, but explained that the title realist had been applied to him just as the title romantic had been applied to the men of 1830, and declined to comment on the appropriateness of a designation which nobody, he had hoped, took very seriously (G. Riat, *Gustave Courbet*, Paris, 1906, p. 132). The novelist Champfleury called his volume of essays which appeared in 1857 in defence of the newly alerted conscience *Le Réalisme*, but the Preface shows how little store he set by the word, which he describes as 'one of those equivocal terms which may be turned to all sorts of uses', and for which he forecasts a life of no more than thirty years (p. 5). Champfleury points out that it was one of the 'nombreuses religions en *isme*' which were thrown up by the revolution of 1848, and one ought to be aware of its political overtones. In response to the accusation that he was a socialist painter, Courbet declared himself 'not only socialist, but even more democrat and republican, in a word supporter of the whole revolution, and above all realist, that is to say sincere friend of the real truth' (G. Riat, *op. cit.*, p. 94). Zola was to make the same identification in his essay 'La République et la Littérature', with the confession that 'au fond des querelles littéraires, il y a toujours une question philosophique' [at the bottom of all literary quarrels there is always a philosophical question] (*RE*, p. 401). And Jules Claretie offered a useful summary a year or two later, saying that the theories of M. Champfleury, the intense poetry of Baudelaire, even the fantasies of Murger and Courbet's painting, had as a framework the political situation of 1848, and that this laying claim to the true might be seen as a parallel phenomenon to the need of reorganization and social reform in those same impassioned times (Crouzet, *Duranty*, p. 53 n.).

It is hardly surprising, therefore, that later writers – particularly those loosely referred to as 'Parnassians', whose concern for form led them to react against this democratization of art as an absurd contradiction – treated the word with derision. Flaubert insisted to George Sand, 'notez que j'exècre ce qu'on est convenu d'appeler le réalisme, bien qu'on m'en fasse un des pontifs' [note that I detest what it is fashionable to call realism, even though they set me up as one of its high priests] (*Correspondance*, VII, p. 285), and Baudelaire, writing on *Madame Bovary* in the year of its appearance (1857), rounded on the word as an 'injure dégoutante jetée à la face de tous les analystes, mot vague et élastique qui signifie pour le vulgaire, non pas une méthode nouvelle de création, mais une description minutieuse des accessoires ... [a disgusting insult thrown in the face of every rational person, a vague and elastic word which signifies for the vulgar not a new method of creation but a minute description of trivialities] (*Oeuvres*, Pléiade ed., Paris, 1954, p. 1007).

But more important than the early realists' unease with the word itself, was their anxiety lest realism should be misunderstood and taken (by 'le vulgaire') for a school or programme. 'Je crains les écoles comme le choléra,' said Champfleury (*Le Réalisme*, p. 272); and Edmond Duranty was even more explicit: 'this terrible word Realism is the reverse of the word school. To say 'realist school' is an absurdity: realism signifies the frank and complete expression of individualities; convention, imitation, and any kind of school, are exactly what it attacks' (cit. Zola, *RE*, p. 307). So realism – the very word entertained on sufferance – is not a movement. Nor is it a method; Champfleury ridicules the idea of a formula which might be taken up by a prospective realist: 'j'avoue n'avoir jamais étudié le code qui contient les lois à l'aide desquelles il est permis au premier venu de produire des oeuvres réalistes' (*Le Réalisme*, p. 272).

Johnson would not define poetry, but he allowed 'it is much easier to say what it is not' (Boswell, 12 April 1776); and one soon realizes that realism as preached and practised at this time is only susceptible of negative definition. Wimsatt and Brooks in their *Literary Criticism* 'use the term broadly to mean a reaction against a number of things that were thought in the mid-nineteenth century to be *un*-real' (p. 456). The realists saw a straightforward alternative between 'le rêve' and 'la réalité', dream and reality. The exposure of this antithesis is a recurrent theme in Zola's work. He declared with typical forthrightness in *Mes Haines* (1866): 'peindre des rêves est un jeu d'enfant et de femme; les hommes ont charge de peindre des réalités' [only children and women dwell on dreams; men should busy themselves with realities] (cit. *RN*, p. 65). Already in *Thérèse Raquin* we have the situation where Thérèse's family moves to the dingy Parisian shop her mother has rented, and 'Madame Raquin, en face de la réalité, resta embarrassée, honteuse de ses rêves'. Laurent confesses to Thérèse, later, 'J'avais un rêve, je voulais passer une nuit entière avec toi, m'endormir dans tes bras et me reveiller le lendemain sous tes baisers. Je vais contenter ce rêve'; but the reality on which this dream of happiness founders is the terrible desiccation of their desire caused by their guilt over the murdered Camille. And at the end of the Rougon-Maquart series, in the novel called *Le Rêve* (1888), Angélique's dream of love is again denied by the oppressive reality of her circumstances.

Duranty expressed the aggressive intentions of realism in announcing 'what it attacks', as we saw above; and his own short-lived review, *Réalisme*, contains some of the most vigorous realist polemic. The violence is adequately suggested by the title alone of one of Duranty's articles, 'Les *Contemplations* de Victor Hugo ou le gouffre géant des sombres abîmes romantiques' [Victor Hugo's *Contemplations*, or the great abyss of romantic melancholy], and the tone by its contents: 'he doesn't like women; he doesn't understand children: he doesn't notice nature'. Duranty's attack became even more random and abusive: 'Edgar Poe is like Dutch cheese and Baudelaire the hermit rat . . . Lamartine is a creole, Musset a shadow of Don Juan, whom he has taken seriously; de Vigny an hermaphrodite' (Crouzet, pp. 69, 72). It is hardly surprising that *Réalisme* only saw six issues. Champfleury describes the realists as 'tired of versified lies, of the persistence of the tail-end romantics', and ridicules the romantic novelist who 'ignores his own time in order to dig up corpses from the past and dress them up in historical frippery' (*Le Réalisme*, pp. 5, 86). These are terms very reminiscent of the rejection of the heroic romance in early eighteenth-century England by writers like Addison and Steele, and later by the novelists themselves. Evidence was amassed endlessly, and sentence was always being passed. Baudelaire had already delivered his in an essay on Pierre Dupont in 1851, where he applauded Dupont's joyousness and reprobated the conventional romantic melancholy:

Disparaissez donc, ombres fallacieuses de René, d'Obermann et de Werther; fuyez dans les brouillards du vide, monstrueuses créations de la paresse et de la solitude; comme les pourceaux dans le lac de Génézareth, allez vous replonger dans les forêts enchantées d'où vous tirèrent les fées ennemis, moutons attaqués du vertigo romantique. Le génie de l'action ne vous laisse plus de place parmi nous.

[Vanish then, deceptive shades of René, Obermann and Werther, vanish into the gaping mists, monstrous creations of idleness and solitude; like the Gadarene swine, plunge back into the enchanted forests where you found your fairytale antagonists, sheep attacked by romantic vertigo. The genius of action no longer allows you a place amongst us.]

(*Oeuvres*, Pléiade ed., p. 968)

Fernand Desnoyers welcomed realism in an article 'Du Réalisme' which appeared in *L'Artiste* in 1855. 'Enfin, le Réalisme Vient!' he declares:

It is through this undergrowth, this battle of the Cimbri, this pandemonium of Greek temples, lyres, and Jew's harps, moorish palaces and sickly oaks, boleros, stupid sonnets, gilded odes, rusty daggers, rapiers, and weekly columns, woodnymphs in the moonlight and love-sick feelings, marriages out of M. Scribe, witty caricatures and natural photographs, canes and collars, toothless discussions and criticisms, tottery traditions, awkward customs and couplets addressed to the public, that realism has made a breach.

The tone is one of derision: 'des gamins de Paris hurlent après les chausses des derniers romantiques' [Paris urchins cry at the heels of the last romantics] (9 December 1855; pp. 199, 198).

But there is no death penalty in the history of ideas, no line ever becomes extinct; and it was no doubt the permanent possibility of a romantic revival that kept alive the realist polemic against romanticism – as we shall see, even into the naturalist phase with the renewed assault by Zola. When the time came round (inevitably) for realism and naturalism themselves to stand in the dock at the end of the century, their dismissal of romanticism was the one thing consistently offered in their defence. In Huysmans' *Là-Bas* (1891), Durtal attacks the naturalist philosophy, but acknowledges 'les inoubliables services que les naturalistes ont rendus à l'art' [the unforgettable services which the naturalists rendered to art]: 'car enfin ce sont eux qui nous ont débarrassés des inhumains fantoches du romantisme et qui ont extrait la littérature d'un idéalisme de ganache et d'une inanition de vieille fille exaltée par le célibat' [because it was they after all who rid us of the artificial puppets of romanticism, who saved literature from worn-out idealism and the futility of an old maid fevered by celibacy] (Livre de Poche ed., p. 6). Edmund Gosse said that realism 'cleared the air of a thousand follies'; Philip Rahv argues that naturalism 'revolutionized writing by liquidating the last assets of "romance" in fiction and by purging it once and for all of the idealism of the "beautiful lie" ' (*DMLR*, pp. 392, 588).

The united front presented against romanticism gave a superficial and deceptive aspect of cohesion to the realist idea; but the annexation of 'la réalité' was not carried out with the same efficiency as the expropriation of 'le rêve'. The appeal made by the realists to truth was essentially simplistic. 'When realism appeals neither to ontological argument nor to scientific experiment but to human experience, philosophers consider it "naïve" ' (Levin, *GH*, p. 65). The importation into the novel of scientific methods did not happen until the second generation of realists (who are for that reason more precisely described as 'naturalists'); the first generation had little more to guide them than their conscience towards the truth, and the operations of this conscience are quite uncomplicated. Bornecque and Cogny describe the impulse of realism as 'un sursaut du besoin de vérité' [a sudden start in the need for truth] (*RN*, p. 18) and sudden starts are often clumsy. Desnoyers bases his statement of faith in realism on the proposition that 'le mot vérité met tout le monde d'accord', and defines it simply as 'la peinture vraie des objets' (*L'Artiste*, p. 197).

With much the same confidence, much later, Theodore Dreiser was to announce (in an article called 'True Art Speaks Plainly') that 'truth is what is' (*DMLR*, p. 155). This is not far from the exposed tautology of Falstaff's 'Is not the truth the truth?' (*1 Henry IV*, II iv 222); and Dreiser's assertion that 'the sum and substance of literary as well as social morality may be expressed in three words – tell the truth' certainly offers no solution to, nor even any useful commentary on, the writer's problems.

The conscientious realist's solution to such problems was to pretend, in fact, that they did not exist. Conscience inhibits consciousness. The obsession with truth does not leave room for an obsession with anything else: questions of technique are ignored, proscribed, as part of the 'literary' paraphernalia of the past. 'The technique of realism', says Harry Levin (catching the word 'technique' in a peculiar stance), 'is iconoclastic' (*GH*, p. 62); and 'to convince us of his essential veracity', he has argued in another place, 'the novelist must always be disclaiming the fictitious and breaking through the encrustations of the literary' ('What is Realism?', *Comparative Literature*, III (1951) 193–9; p. 196). The realist aesthetic, then (if it may be called such), is consistently reductive; questions of form are obliterated in the more pressing concern of content. Champfleury uses the argument from translation to prove to his own satisfaction 'l'infériorité de la forme et la puissance de l'idée' (*Le Réalisme*, p. 16), and summarily divides all writers into 'sincéristes' and 'formistes' as they uphold or do not uphold the realist idea (*GH*, p. 70).

This explains the realists' 'haine vigoureuse' of poetry (Champfleury), a hatred anticipated by Coleridge when he wrote, 'poetry is not the proper antithesis to prose, but to science' (Nonesuch, *Coleridge*, p. 313). Poetry offended Courbet's democratic instincts: 'it's dishonest to write poetry, pretentious to express yourself differently from other people'; and aroused the wrath of Duranty, who saw it as 'an infirmity, a sickly secretion of hemistiches which gather in a rotten brain and leak out more or less painfully' (Crouzet, *Duranty*, p. 69). Desnoyers was more conciliatory in an open letter to Champfleury: 'Soyons poètes en vers et réalistes en prose' (*Figaro*, 9 Nov. 1856).

One way of describing the continuous revolution of ideal and value in literature would be to see it as an alternation between complexity and simplicity, where now self-consciousness and sophistication and now unconsciousness and sincerity seem to be the only things worth striving for. The realists were in reaction against complexity, consciousness, and so simplicity and sincerity came to be seen by them as criteria of worth (that is, preconditions of realism) in artistic production – 'simplicity' which is scarcely less of an equivocation than realism itself, and 'sincerity', as Stravinsky said, 'the *sine qua non* which yet guarantees nothing'. Champfleury declared that sincerity was the only thing he valued in art, and went on to confess his liking for 'la poésie populaire avec ses rimes en gros sabots at ses sentiments naturels' [popular poetry with its clumsy hobnailed rhymes and its plain feelings] (*Le Réalisme*, pp. 3, 18). Here at least form isn't all-important. Duranty interprets the realist programme in a very similar way: 'realism commits itself to an exact, complete, and sincere reproduction of the social milieu, of the contemporary world . . . this reproduction should therefore be as simple as possible so that anyone may understand it.'

Zola quotes this passage in his enthusiastic essay 'Le Réalisme' on Duranty's journal in *Le Roman Expérimental* (p. 307), and it is Zola himself who formulates the reductive principle of realistic technique most clearly in his metaphor of the three screens, 'les trois écrans'. One may consider it here without introducing Zola's ideas prematurely, because Zola developed this metaphor in a long letter to a friend in August 1864 – before he had published a novel, and well before the official launching of naturalism with the Rougon Macquart series (1871–93). In this letter Zola elaborates a scheme to take account of different points of view, different aspects of reality, which reads rather like Henry James's 1909 preface to *The Portrait of a Lady*: 'the House of fiction has in short not one window, but a million . . . ' (*AN*, p. 46). But Zola is more concerned to justify a particular position ('toutes mes sympathies, s'il faut le dire, sont pour l'Écran réaliste') and so he describes how the classic screen is enlarging, 'un verre grandissant', the romantic screen distorts – 'l'Écran romantique est . . . un prisme', whereas the realist screen gives an unimpeded view: 'l'Écran réaliste est un simple verre à vitre, très mince, très clair, et qui a la prétention d'être si parfaitement transparent que les images le transversent et se reproduisent ensuite dans leur réalité' [the realist screen is plain glass, very thin, very clear, which aspires to be so perfectly transparent that images may pass through it and remake themselves in all their reality].

Zola appreciates the implausibility of the metaphor ('Il est, certes, difficile de caractériser un Écran qui a pour qualité principale celle de n'être presque pas' [I agree it's difficult to describe a screen whose distinguishing quality is that it scarcely exists]) and he does actually go on to concede that all screens must distort to a certain extent. Zola's screen which will 'n'être presque pas' is just as chimerical as Flaubert's subject which should become 'presque invisible'. In one case it is the form, and in the other the content that seeks to purify itself by burning away the other – and neither purity may ever be attained. One would make expression unnecessary, and the other impossible. But the kind of impossibility striven towards will nevertheless determine in some measure the kind of book that it does in each case prove possible to write. And the conflicting ambitions expressed in these two attitudes will explain Flaubert's impatience with Zola, writing to Turgenev in 1876: ' . . . Lisez ses feuilletons du lundi, vous verrez comme il croit avoir découvert 'le Naturalisme!' Quant à la poésie et au style, qui sont les deux éléments éternels, jamais il n'en parle' [If you read his articles on Mondays you will see how he thinks he has discovered 'Naturalism!' As for poetry and style, which are the two eternal elements, he never even mentions them] (*Correspondance*, VII, p. 369).

But the most significant element in the uncertain fabric of realist theory at this stage, and that which contains the most serious implications, is its habitual suspicion of the imagination. As early as 1845 P. Limayrac complained that if the imagination had 'played an important and enriching role in the modern school', it was also true that it had 'deceived our hopes' (Crouzet, *Duranty*, p. 51). This disenchantment really underlies everything else. The reaction against the lies and dreams of the romantics and the promulgation of a reductive aesthetic are both symptomatic of a crisis of confidence in the imagination – a crisis which entails a systematic repudiation of its function. One is even tempted to see the very vigour of the invective directed against the romantics – the inventiveness of the disparagement, as with Desnoyer's vision of the Paris urchins' abuse – as a curious case of the imagination taking revenge on itself, submitting to some kind of self-administered humiliation.

Diderot is one of the writers over whom Champfleury enthuses in his promulgation of realism. And it is interesting to observe the terms in which he praises one of his novels, the *Histoire de Mademoiselle de la Chaux*: 'Diderot didn't invent anything, discover anything, or imagine anything; he was only the intelligent copyist of an unfortunate passion that played itself before him; he had to do no more than display human nature in a certain number of pages' (*Le Réalisme*, pp. 94–5).

And here one must anticipate Zola's treatment of the imagination, if only because he states the realist case (as usual) most uncompromisingly; although one has the additional reason that it is in their attitude towards the imagination, as towards those creatures of imagination the romantics, that the two phases of conscientious realism evince their kinship most clearly.

Zola's definitive 'placing' of the imagination occurs in the short chapter 'Le Sens du Réel' from 'Du Roman' (*RE*, pp. 205–12) where he argues that the imaginative faculty has been superseded by other faculties in the modern novelist, and may even prove a distraction when he gets down to writing his work. 'The highest praise one could formerly make of a novelist was to say: "he has imagination". Now that praise would almost be regarded as a criticism. This is because the conditions of the novel have changed. Imagination is no longer the novelist's most important faculty.' Zola allows imagination to Dumas, Eugène Sue, Hugo, and George Sand: this is all part of his strategy. For he then denies that one need invoke the imagination to describe the work of Balzac and Stendhal; or the work of Flaubert, the Goncourts, Daudet: 'their talent does not depend on their imagination, but on the fact that they render nature with intensity'. And so, he goes on, 'I insist on this abasement of the imagination, because I see here the essential characteristic of the modern novel'; there could hardly be a more deliberate and uncompromising dismissal than this. There was a time, he agrees, when the imagination had a function; this was when the novel was merely a recreation or amusement. But now, 'with the naturalist novel, the novel of observation and analysis, conditions have changed . . . the writer's whole effort is directed towards obliterating the imaginary with the real'. Finally he confesses that Balzac's imagination irritates rather than delights him – and precisely because of Balzac's confidence, his ambition to create the world anew: ' . . . l'imagination de Balzac, cette imagination déréglée qui se jetait dans toutes les exagérations et qui voulait créer le monde à nouveau, sur des plans extraordinaires, cette imagination m'irrite plus qu'elle ne m'attire'.

Zola's relegation of the imagination in this essay cannot but bring to mind Plato's expulsion of the poet from the ideal state in *The Republic*.

Then apparently if there comes to our city a man so wise that he can turn into everything under the sun and imitate every conceivable object, when he offers to show off himself and his poems to us, we shall do obeisance to him as to a sacred, wonderful, and agreeable person; but we shall say that we have no such man in our city, and the law forbids there being one, and we shall anoint him with myrrh, and crown him with a wreath of sacred wool, and send him off to another city, and for ourselves we shall employ a more austere and less attractive poet and story-teller, whose poetry will be to our profit . . .

(trans. A. D. Lindsay; Everyman ed., London, 1954, p. 80)

This is a result of the 'ancient quarrel between philosophy and poetry' (p. 311), the quarrel between different kinds of truth. Plato had the same conscience as Zola towards the truth (though they would not of course have agreed as to what the truth was). Both confess to a reluctant admiration for the transforming power of the imagination, but both are primarily suspicious of it and insist that art should disdain its meretricious wiles and suffer itself to be 'chastiz'd to Truth'. Plato requires that poetry, to justify itself, should become 'more austere and less attractive'; Zola suggests that the novel should no longer distract us with an exotic subject-matter: 'au contraire, plus elle sera banale et générale, plus elle deviendra typique' [on the contrary, the more banal and generalized it is, the more typical it will become]. This is the condition of 'passive and silent' objectivity with which Hector Agosti associates 'the old realism' (*DMLR*, p. 495).

There is a paragraph in the preface to Émile de Vogüé's *Le Roman Russe* (1886) which will provide an excellent summary of the ideas I have dealt with so far in this chapter. De Vogüé considers the effects of the replacement of classical theories of art:

Almost unnoticed during the last century other views have come to be accepted. They have brought about an art of observation rather than of imagination, one which boasts that it observes life as it is in its wholeness and complexity with the least possible prejudice on the part of the artist. It takes men under ordinary conditions, shows characters in the course of their everyday existence, average and changing. Jealous of the rigour of scientific procedure, the writer proposes to instruct us by a perpetual analysis of feelings and of acts rather than to divert us or move us by intrigue and exhibition of the passions. Classical art imitated a king who governed, punished, rewarded, chose his favourites among an aristocratic élite, and imposed on them conventions of elegance, morality, and seemly speech. The new art seeks to imitate nature in its unconsciousness, its moral indifference, its lack of choice; it expresses the triumph of the group over the individual, of the crowd over the hero, of the relative over the absolute. It has been called realist, naturalist: would democratic not offer an adequate definition? (pp. xiv–xv)

II

In considering Zola's essay I have run on inevitably into the more sharply defined arena of naturalism; and the comments of both de Vogüé and Agosti refer to the whole realist/naturalist phenomenon. It is legitimate to speak of the two in one breath – Edmond de Goncourt does so in his preface to *Les Frères Zemganno* (1879) – and many writers are content to consider them as synonyms or near-synonyms. In England particularly we have been reluctant to make any distinction: a translation of Huysman's *Là-Bas* – complete with critical appendages – gives 'realism' as a translation of 'naturalisme' throughout the important argument between Durtal and Des Hermies about naturalism in the first chapter of the novel. (The Fortune Press: undated, but *c.* 1930). Commenting on his own use of the word in his recent book *The Pre-Raphaelite Imagination* (London, 1968), John Dixon Hunt says 'in France the terms *realism* and *naturalism* represented different approaches and creative methods, but with their importation into England the distinction was blurred and becomes less useful' (p. 211 n.).

But it would be misleading to confuse the two terms simply because each may be applied to a similar kind of book. Especially since there is one obvious way to distinguish them: 'realism' derives from philosophy and describes an *objective*, the attainment of the real; 'naturalism' derives from natural philosophy or science and describes a *method* which shall conduce to the attainment of the real. Admittedly usage does not always make this clear; realism is spoken of as a technique, and naturalism as a tendency; but it will be useful to keep in mind the different kind of description involved when one is interpreting – or using – these words.

I have said that naturalism may be more sharply defined, and the fact that it describes a method is the main reason for this. Realism had faltered (there is a parallel in the fortunes of the revolution) – at least it had never developed. There was nothing to follow up the anti-romantic offensive. Conscience alone was not enough; the endless professions of 'simplicity' and 'sincerity' expressed goodwill but did not provide good works. This was of course the most serious impediment: the non-appearance of the significant work that should embody realist ideas and prove that these were not simply destructive precursors (as actually they are) of 'l'alittérature', anti-literature. The realists, it is true, laid claim to *Madame Bovary*, but Flaubert disclaimed realism. They courted Baudelaire, but were again repulsed. The spirit was willing but the flesh was weak; realism needed a more positive definition, a more specific objective, if it was not to diffuse itself (and endure in its turn a reaction) before its own fulfilment.

This fulfilment was achieved by the naturalist initiative, which followed the pointers in realist theory to their logical conclusion and provided a scientific method to carry out its programme. 'Le naturalisme continue le réalisme, l'affirme et l'exagère' says P. Martino (*Le Naturalisme français (1870–95)*, p. 1). According to Philip Rahv, naturalism is 'an extreme emphasis in the general onset of realistic fiction and drama' (*DMLR*, p. 588); for Harry Levin 'the last prolongation of realism' (*GH*, p. 463). Bornecque and Cogny look on realism as a feeble anticipation of naturalism which becomes hardened and systematized on the way towards its goal (*RN*, pp. 36, 18).

Naturalism hardened itself by compact with the age, and systematized itself by submitting to the discipline of science. The early realists had also made some attempt to see themselves in the context of their age – especially in politics, as we have seen; and the enthusiastic Champfleury drew parallels in other areas. 'Everyone who introduces some new idea gets called a realist. We will soon be seeing realist doctors, realist chemists, realist manufacturers, realist historians.' His simple apology for realism – 'l'époque le veut ainsi' – directly anticipates Zola's studied deference to the spirit of the age (*Le Réalisme*, pp. 272, 276). But the identification was not yet so complete, nor so confidently asserted. In a sense it could not be, because there was less that could be specifically identified with. Science had, it is true, already announced its ambitions, and reasserted its faith in the empirical approach to knowledge as this had been elaborated in the seventeenth and eighteenth centuries. Comte had claimed in his *Cours de Philosophie Positive* (1830–42) that the progress of science was systematically reducing the area of our ignorance, and Ernest Renan had accepted the implication of the new spirit of science for literature in his youthful declaration of faith, *L'Avenir de la Science* (1848–9):

> The real world that science reveals to us is by far superior to the fantastic world created by the imagination . . . it is futile to inflate our ideas, to sacrifice the reality of things for the mere fragments we have brought forth . . . if the marvels of fiction have always seemed necessary to poetry, the marvels of nature, when revealed in all their splendour, will constitute a poetry a thousand times more sublime, a poetry which will be reality itself, which will be at the same time science and philosophy.
>
> (*Oeuvres Complètes*, ed. Henriette Psichari, Paris, 1949; III, 804–5)

'Tout est vanité, excepté la science,' he wrote in a letter at the same time; 'l'art même commence à me paraître un peu vide' (*RN*, p. 47).

But the real scientific achievements which would vindicate these ambitions – turn these scientific dreams into realities – were yet to come. (It is significant that Renan called his book *The Future of Science*.) Darwin's *The Origin of Species* in 1859 was the classic example of an important scientific work that fulfilled an earlier promise – realizing in its evidence for the theory of evolution ideas already entertained by Diderot in his *Le Rêve de d'Alembert* (1769). Claude Bernard's *Introduction à l'Étude de la Médecine Expérimentale*, which was to be Zola's main source for the scientific method, appeared in 1865. And the influence of Comte's positivism was only now – in the 1860s and later – being recognized and applied in literature, mainly through the discipleship of Taine. If realism was on the way to becoming in art what positivism was in philosophy, as Brunetière wrote in *Le Roman Naturaliste* (1883), then in its naturalist apotheosis it realized this condition.

There is an important shift of emphasis to be remarked here also. Empiricism in its origins had been sceptical; in the *Advancement of Learning* (1605) Bacon was concerned to fight clear of all kinds of dogmatism. But during the nineteenth century this scepticism gave way, under the incitement of 'l'orgueil de tout comprendre', the pride of knowing everything (*RN*, p. 45), to a new dogma, the dogma of determinism; a 'mind-forged manacle' of more modern design but of equal disrepute with the intellectual tyrannies of the past. One recalls what John Stuart Mill – himself shy of systems – had to say in his *Autobiography* about Comte's projected 'Système de Politique Positive': 'the completest system of spiritual and temporal despotism which ever yet emanated from a human brain, unless possibly that of Ignatius Loyola' (ch. 6). The writers of the time were to become infected only too readily by this confidence, and Zola – a principal culprit – underlined the essential difference between the empirical and the fully-fledged scientific phase with due enthusiasm in *Le Roman Expérimental*: 'tout est devenu scientifique, et l'empiricisme a disparu' he repeats on the

authority of Bernard; and proceeds to argue himself that 'l'empir-
isme précède fatalement l'état scientifique d'une connaissance'
[everything has become scientific, empiricism has disappeared . . .
empiricism inevitably precedes the scientific stage of any know-
ledge] (*RE*, pp. 23, 38).

III

It was Taine who first argued the naturalist theory in literature, in
the introduction to his *Histoire de la Littérature Anglaise* (1863–4),
and it will be useful to consider his main ideas before passing on to
Zola.

Taine sought to drain off mystery from the mind of man, and to
bring all subjects of study into the scientific phase. The universe
was a great mechanism, and everything – including man, his moral
life, and all his works – could be understood in terms of cause and
effect.

> The research into causes must come after the collection of facts. It
> doesn't matter whether the facts are physical or moral, they will still
> have causes; there are causes for ambition, courage, and truthfulness
> as there are for digestion, muscular movement, and animal warmth.
> Vice and virtue are products like vitriol and sugar, and every complex
> element has its origins in the admixture of other, simpler, elements on
> which it depends.
>
> (vol. I, p. xv)

The complexity that was literature had its own simpler causes too,
and it is Taine's main argument in this preface to discover these in
the three conditions of 'la race, le milieu, et le moment'; heredity,
environment, and immediate circumstances. He goes so far as to
claim that when we have exhausted examination of these, 'we have
exhausted not only all the actual causes, but even all the possible
causes' (p. xxxiii). People misunderstood Stendhal, says Taine,
because he was the first to compose his novels by a scientific pro-

cedure; they did not understand that 'he introduced scientific procedures into the history of the heart: calculation, simplification, deduction; that he was the first to record the elementary causes . . . in short, that he dealt with the feelings as one should deal with them, that is to say as a naturalist and as a physicist' (p. xliv). Taine's essay on Balzac contains a developed image of Balzac as a naturalist, disdaining the facilities of the imagination and labouring away at his scientific task, 'péniblement et obstinément enfoncé dans son fumier de science', and emerging with the smell of the laboratory; his work is (with that of Shakespeare and Saint-Simon) 'le plus grand magasin de documents que nous ayons sur la nature humaine' [the greatest hoard of information which we have on human nature] (*Nouveaux Essais*, 1865, pp. 118, 170).

Ideas, like religions, require their saints, and Taine was not the first to claim Balzac as the 'great progenitor' of naturalism. The preface of 1842 to the *Comédie Humaine* was the sacred text; there Balzac himself drew the parallel between man in society and the animal kingdom in nature: 'je vis que . . . la société ressemblait à la nature. La société ne fait-elle pas de l'homme, suivant les milieux où son action se déploie, autant d'hommes différents qu'il y a de variétés en zoologie?' [I saw that society resembled nature. Does not society make of man, according to the environment in which his life is lived out, as many different kinds of men as there are species in zoology?] (*Oeuvres Complètes*, 1901; *Scènes de la Vie Privée*, II, p. 82). One character-study, 'Monographe du Rentier', actually begins with a paragraph of scientific classification in the required style:

Rentier – Anthropomorphe selon Linné, mammifère selon Cuvier, genre de l'ordre des parisiens, famille des actionnaires, tribu des ganaches, le *civis inermis* des anciens, découvert par l'abbé Terray, observé par Silhouette, maintenu par Turgot et Necker, définitivement établi aux dépens des 'producteurs' de Saint-Simon par le grand – livre.

[Man of independent means – treated as human according to Linnaeus, mammal according to Cuvier, genus of the category of Parisians, family of shareholders, tribe of blockheads, the 'harmless citizen' of ancient times, discovered by Father Terray, studied by Silhouette, kept by Turgot and Necker, definitively established by the ledger at the expense of Saint-Simon's 'workers'].

(*Oeuvres Diverses*, I, p. 1)

and although there is obviously an ironic intention here (the passage reminds one of Bitzer's definition of a horse in *Hard Times*: ' "Quadruped. Graminivorous. Forty teeth, namely twenty-four grinders, four eye-teeth, and twelve incisive. Sheds coat in the spring; in marshy countries, sheds hoofs too ... " ') Balzac is being straightforward when he says, 'La société française allait être l'historien, je ne devais être que le secrétaire ... ' [French society was to be the historian, I was going to be merely the secretary] (I, p. 84). His intention is, he says, to emulate Buffon's work on zoology, and write a natural history of man: although it must be remarked that Balzac at the same time deliberately dissociates himself from 'l'école sensualiste et matérialiste' (II, p. 88), the sensualist and materialist philosophy that was to provide the real impetus for naturalism.

The Goncourts could now confidently present the novelist as a fully-fledged scientist, as they do in the preface to *Germinie Lacerteux* (1864): 'Aujourd'hui que le Roman ... devient, par l'analyse et par la recherche psychologique, l'Histoire moral contemporaine, aujourd'hui que le Roman s'est imposé les études et les devoirs de la science, il peut en revendiquer les libertés et les franchises' [now that the novel has become, by analysis and by psychological study, contemporary moral history, now that the novel has taken upon itself the researches and the duties of science, it may lay claim to a similar freedom and immunity] (p. viii). It was Taine's words 'Le vice et le vertu sont des produits, comme le vitriol et le sucre' that Zola used as an epigraph to the first edition of *Thérèse Raquin* (1868), and Taine who inspired the ideas in the preface Zola wrote – reluctantly – for the second edition, declaring that his object was primarily a scientific one: 'I have simply done on two living bodies the work of analysis which surgeons perform on corpses' (Livre de Poche ed., Paris, 1968, pp. 8, 9).

And so all art aspires to the condition of science; by 1870, certainly, Coleridge's 'shaping spirit of Imagination' had been replaced by the 'shaping strength' of science (the phrase comes in Roland Stromberg's translation of part of Emil du Bois-Reymond's *Natural Science and the History of Culture* (1878); *RNS*, p. 30).

IV

Zola was the self-appointed theorist as well as the leading exponent of what he called 'la formule naturaliste', and the essays collected in *Le Roman Expérimental* (1880) represent the completest critical account of naturalism.

As I have said, the realist conscience had not been satisfied by the first fusillade against the romantics, and the need to castigate falsity was an important detonator of Zola's theory. His 'Lettre à la Jeunesse' moves from a criticism of Hugo's poetry and the writings of Ernest Renan (who had gone soft, according to Zola, and surrendered his scientific spirit to the temptations of his own obscurantist rhetoric) to a vigorous attack on the falsifying verbiage of romanticism. Romanticism and lyricism, he says, 'invest everything in words. Words swell to fill the whole picture, and finally give way under the baroque exaggeration of the idea . . . it is a verbal construct built on nothing. There you have romanticism' (*RE*, p. 65). He describes the romantic movement feelingly as 'une pure émeute de rhétoriciens' [a simple riot of rhetoricians]. But the essay also contains what distinguishes it from the critical offensives of Duranty and Champfleury: an emphatic positive, the advocacy of an alternative. Zola invokes Claude Bernard, 'l'incarnation de la vérité affirmée et prouvée', as a contrast to Hugo and Renan, and insists that artists must submit themselves to a similar rigour, abandon the unknown for the known. Science has all the promise: 'it is science that makes idealism retreat before it, science that prepares the twentieth century'. And so he proposes his programme for the young on whom France depends: 'plus de lyrisme, plus de grands mots vides, mais des faits, des documents' [no more lyricism, no more big empty words, but facts, documents]; 'believe only in facts,' he urges, 'the only need now is the strength of truth' (*RE*, pp. 85–6, 96, 104, 60).

It is its firm, declared faith in science, in the methods of observation, experimentation, and documentation, that really characterizes the naturalist idea. Naturalism is quite simply 'la formule de la science moderne appliquée à la littérature'. Zola's most important essay, 'Le Roman Expérimental' (*RE*, pp. 1–53), is a determined identification of the writer's task with that of the scientist: 'we are working with the rest of the age on the great work which is the conquest of nature, with man's power increased tenfold' (p. 29). His confidence in the scientific method is unreserved. It is the *only* method, which must draw all disciplines after it. 'The return to nature, the naturalist evolution which is carrying the century away, is slowly leading all the expressions of human intelligence in a scientific direction' (p. 1). The novel must set a good example by submitting to the scientific spirit. 'Science is making its way into our world'; Zola will draw the novel like a wooden horse into the citadel of art, and effect its liberation from 'les folies des poètes et des philosophes' (pp. 16, 37).

Scientific objectives can only be attained by scientific methods. 'Tout se réduit ... à une question de méthode,' says Zola to conclude his arguments: it all comes down to a question of method. Naturalism took its name from science – the naturalist as observer of natural phenomena – as an earnest of its intention to make its whole labour parallel, indeed part of, scientific inquiry in general;

and Zola fulfilled this intention in his crucial analogy between the novelist and the doctor. He had already compared himself to a 'chirurgien', a surgeon, in the preface to *Thérèse Raquin*: but now he had open before him Claude Bernard's *Introduction à l'Étude de la Médecine Expérimentale*, and he worked out the details of the identification with great literalness. He saw it simply as a matter of writing 'novelist' where Bernard wrote 'doctor': 'le plus souvent, il me suffira de remplacer le mot "médecin" par le mot "romancier" pour rendre ma pensée claire et lui apporter la rigeur d'une vérité scientifique' (p. 2). The intellectual and spiritual are subsumed in the physical; this is of course the conclusion of materialist philosophy, after Taine, which Zola summarizes in an important passage which prepares for the uncompromising state-ment, 'Un même déterminisme doit régir la pierre des chemins et le cerveau de l'homme' [The same determinism controls the stones on the road and the mind of man].

Quand on aura prouvé que le corps de l'homme est une machine, dont on pourra un jour démonter et remonter les rouages au gré de l'expérimentateur, il faudra bien passer aux actes passionels et intel-lectuels de l'homme. Dès lors, nous entrerons dans le domaine qui, jusqu'à présent, appartenait à la philosophie et à la littérature; ce sera la conquête décisive par la science des hypothèses des philosophes et des écrivains.

[When we have proved that man's body is a machine, whose parts the experimenter will one day be able to take to pieces and put together again at will, we shall have to pass to his mind and passions. And from then on we shall be in the realm which has always been considered the right of philosophy and literature; this will represent the decisive conquest by science over the hypotheses of philosophers and writers.]

(p. 15)

Zola faces the question of whether the experimental method is in fact applicable in literature – 'l'expérience est-elle possible?'[1] – but his answer is once again a compound of analogy and assertion.

[1] 'Expérience' can mean either an experience or an experiment.

He declares that Balzac's *Cousine Bette* is simply the trial of the experience, conducted before the eyes of the public: 'simplement le procès-verbal de l'expérience, que le romancier répète sous les yeux du public' (p. 8); the novelist becomes a 'juge d'instruction' or inquisitor. Another metaphor Zola repeats from Bernard – 'Il écoute la nature, et il écrit sous sa dictée' (p. 6) brings to mind Balzac's description of himself as the 'secretary' to French society. And so Zola has satisfied himself that a genuine 'experiment' takes place. The novelist is both observer (empirical) and experimenter (scientific): the observer prepares the ground where characters may appear and things may happen, then the scientist appears and begins the experiment; sets the characters in motion in a particular story (p. 7). The metaphor of experiment does at least involve the idea of an *activity*, the novelist has at least to 'faire mouvoir' his characters. But this activity is still firmly detained in the confines of science; there is no question of the imagination –or of poetry or style, Flaubert's 'eternal principles' – returning through a back door. Zola maintains that questions of method and questions of style are independent (p. 46); the contrast with Flaubert's ideas, in point of theory, could not be more complete.

It is remarkable that for all his exaggerated deference to Bernard, Zola chose – or was forced – to dissent from him on one very material point. Bernard had disallowed Zola's straightforward analogy in advance, by pointing out that, in art, 'personality directs everything. There it is a matter of the spontaneous creation of the mind, and that has nothing at all in common with the documentation of natural phenomena, among which the mind must not introduce anything of its own' (p. 48). Zola takes this as an example of the scientist's misunderstanding of art, his reluctance to *trust* it alongside him, and contradicts Bernard's sober distinction with his own unshakeable faith: 'déterminisme domine tout', in art as well as science.

And so intuition/imagination is replaced by observation/experiment; we arrive at the situation where the novelist becomes a technician and his novel a product, which 's'établira de lui-même' – will simply fall into place when all the research has been completed and the facts assembled. The novel has been offered up to ease the conscience of art.

v

Realism, in the sense in which I have been treating it in this chapter, reminds us all the time of its ultimate etymological derivation from *res*, 'thing'. (Harry Levin uses the word 'chosisme', 'thing-ism', as a variant form (*GH*, p. 452).) It arose out of an appeal to the evident truth of the external world and sustained itself by the discipline and privilege of science. It is hardly surprising, therefore, that the crisis of confidence in the scientific account of reality which occurred late in the nineteenth century involved in its turn the discrediting of realism: the realism which 'exalts Life and diminishes Art, exalts things and diminishes words', as Robert Scholes describes it in his recent book *The Fabulators* (p. 11). Crouzet says that Duranty saw in 'materialism', and with good reason, the Achilles' heel of realism (*Duranty*, p. 70), and it was indeed the criticism of its implied philosophy that undermined the simple structure of conscientious realism.

Émile de Vogüé describes the disillusion with science in *Le Roman Russe*: man realized that 'in extending his domain, he had extended his outlook, and . . . beyond the circle of newly conquered truths the abyss of ignorance reappeared, just as vast, just as irritating as before'. And so 'sa présomption extravagante s'évanouit', his extravagant presumption vanished (pp. xx, xxi). More remarkable, however, is the expression of a very similar idea by Ernest Renan himself. Renan had written *L'Avenir de la Science* in 1848–9, but refrained from publishing it until 1890, when he added a preface that submitted his earlier scientific enthusiasm to a very sober criticism. He warns the reader, 'The error that runs through these pages ... is an exaggerated optimism'; because 'even though, through the incessant labour of the nineteenth century, our knowledge of facts has been dramatically increased, human destiny has become more obscure than ever' (*op. cit.*, pp. 720, 726). The early realists had ridiculed the romantics as dreamers; the revolution is complete when in the first surrealist manifesto André Breton can in his turn ridicule 'la rêverie scientifique' on which the art of the realists had depended (*Manifestes du Surréalisme*, Paris, 1962, p. 62).

'Naturalism ... is the logical result of realism, and, by exaggeration, makes the defects and limitations of realism more apparent,' wrote Hamilton Wright Mabie in 1885 (*DMLR*, p. 305). The very fact that naturalism had declared itself so unequivocally made its position untenable when the scientific substructure collapsed, and quickly led to the discrediting of the realist idea in general in so far as it depended on external philosophical support. One is not convinced by Zola's claim to have discovered the naturalist formula working already in the eighteenth century, and even from the beginning of time, or by his protestation that naturalism is not a school (*RE*, pp. 88, 93); nor by Leopoldo Alas's insistence that 'naturalism is not subject to positivism...' (from his preface to the second edition of Emilia Bazan's *La cuéstion palpitante*, 1891; *DMLR*, p. 268). To mingle friendship far is mingling blood, and the propagandists of naturalism had committed it far too deeply to the prevailing philosophy ever to be able to float the idea on its own after this had been challenged.

When Huysmans dramatized the argument over naturalism in *Là-Bas*, he let his character des Hermies direct his main attack on precisely this question of its philosophy.

> ... Ce que je reproche au naturalisme, ce n'est pas le lourd badigeon de son gros style, c'est l'immondice de ses idées; ce que je lui reproche, c'est d'avoir incarné le matérialisme dans la littérature, d'avoir glorifié la démocratie de l'art!

[What I object to in naturalism is not the lumpy wash of its clumsy style, but its garbage of ideas; I object to its having realized materialism in literature, and having glorified the democracy of art.]

'Quelle théorie de cerveau mal famé, quel miteux et étroit système,' he continues; what a low-minded theory, what a shabby restricted system (Livre de Poche ed., p. 1). Flaubert had written to Turgenev in the same spirit: 'ce matérialisme m'indigne, et, presque tous les lundis, j'ai un accès d'irritation en lisant les feuilletons de ce brave Zola. Après les Réalistes, nous avons les Naturalistes et les Impressionistes. Quel progrès! Tas de farceurs … ' [This materialism infuriates me and I react violently nearly every Monday when I read Zola's pamphlets. After the realists, we have the naturalists and the impressionists. What progress! A crowd of practical jokers …] (*Correspondance*, VII, p. 359).

Naturalism suffered, as Huysmans saw very clearly, from being a 'logical result', trapped in the perversity of its own theoretical ideas: 'le naturalisme confiné dans les monotones études d'êtres médiocres, évoluant parmi d'interminables inventaires de salons et des champs, conduisait tout droit à la stérilité la plus complète, si l'on était honnête ou clairvoyant et, dans le cas contraire, aux plus fastidieux des rabâchages, aux plus fatigantes de redites' [naturalism confined to the monotonous studies of mediocre characters, revolving among interminable descriptions of drawing rooms and landscapes, led, if one was honest or farseeing, straight to an utter sterility, and if one was not, to the most tedious reiteration, exhausting and useless repetition]. The ascetic exclusion of the imagination could have only debilitating effects, lead to an art where the novelist would only be hiding 'l'incomparable disette de ses idées sous un ahurissement voulu du style' [the incomparable poverty of his ideas under a deliberate obscurity of style] (pp. 7–8).

There is abundant evidence for the growing impatience felt for naturalist and simpler realist ideas towards the end of the century, and 'le trivialisme' which they seemed to have encouraged in literature. Some of the views expressed will have a more natural place in the next chapter. One might summarize by saying that certain older realizations about imitation and art re-established themselves. On an earlier revolution of the cycle, in the eighteenth century, when the novel was enjoying domestic quiet having driven romance from the gates of its new estate, Johnson voiced the general suspicion that the satisfaction might be premature, and the new order have its own disadvantages: 'If the world be promiscuously described, I cannot see of what use it can be to read the account; or why it may not be as safe to turn the eye immediately upon mankind as upon a mirror which shows all that presents itself without discrimination' (*Rambler*, no. 4). And one revolution later, James may be our spokesman, as with the lessons of twenty novels behind him he laments 'the old burden of the much life and the little art', and faces up once again to 'the fatal futility of Fact' (*AN*, pp. 259, 122).

3
Conscious Realism

I

The usual meaning of realism was, and is, that provided by the realist movement (or tendency) of the third quarter of the nineteenth century. The semantic adventures enjoyed by realism since that time are due to the fact that the word refused to die – or that critics, recognizing its usefulness, refused to let it pass into honourable retirement and await that melancholy event. Naturalism they did discharge: it had collaborated shamelessly with science and its loyalty could hardly be relied upon in the new dispensation. But realism was another matter. A true daughter of Criticism as Johnson describes her – 'a goddess easy of access and forward of advance' (*Idler*, no. 60) – realism had made herself indispensable with her good looks and promise of performance; and now she proved only too willing to demonstrate her versatility by satisfying the expectations of various suitors at the same time. Realism had to be found a place, that was obvious; and this is how the unlikely fact occurred of her retention in the establishment of Idealism.

II

'Peindre, non la chose, mais l'effet qu'elle produit,' wrote the 22-year-old Mallarmé to Henri Cazalis in 1864: paint, not the thing, but the effect that it produces; and this may be seen as a kind of notice of redundancy to the material world, to the stuff of science, which was to take effect later in the century. Of course poetry tends more naturally to retain, independent of philosophical fashion, a kind of instinctive idealism; it was for this reason that the early realists rejected it so completely, saw it as 'une infirmité'. One of Baudelaire's undated papers, a skeletonic disparagement of Champfleury's realism, contains the notes: 'la Poésie est qu'il y a de plus réel, c'est ce qui n'est complètement vrai que dans un autre monde. Ce monde-ci, dictionnaire hiéroglyphique' [poetry is the most real thing we have, what is only made completely real in another world. This world is a dictionary of hieroglyphics] (*Oeuvres*, Pléiade ed., p. 993). Transcendentalism involves idealism and expresses itself ultimately as symbolism in literature.

But the mood of dissatisfaction with the 'inanimate cold world' of Coleridge's 'Dejection Ode' made itself felt outside poetry too, in art generally and eventually in the novel itself. Schopenhauer's pessimism had been an incitement to the naturalists; but more fully understood, his philosophy of art led actually in another direction. 'Schopenhauer's philosophy is an aesthetic gnosis, a secular apocalypse: the world is worthless; art is good. Life is no life; letters are the real thing' (Erich Heller; *DMLR*, p. 593). W. S. Lilly invoked Schopenhauer in the course of an article attacking naturalism in 1885: 'Rightly has Schopenhauer conceived of the function of art . . . as the deliverance of man from the chain of vulgar realities which binds us to this phenomenal world' (*DMLR*, p. 290). It was the novel that had immersed itself most unreservedly in 'this phenomenal world', but its deliverance was at hand. It was in his chapter on Mallarmé in *The Symbolist Movement in Literature* (1899) that Arthur Symons spoke out against the 'old, objective simplicity', and declared that 'the world, which we can no longer believe in as the satisfying material object it was to our grandparents, becomes transfigured with a new light' (p. 137); but he went on in the next chapter to include Huysmans among the symbolist writers, and welcome the 'ideal' novel:

> Here, then, purged of the distraction of incident, liberated from the bondage of a too realistic conversation, in which the aim had been to

convey the very gesture of breathing life, internalized to a complete liberty, in which, just because it is so deliberately free, art is able to accept, without limiting itself, the expressive medium of a convention, we have in the novel a new form . . .

(p. 145)

The phrase 'internalized to a complete liberty' – in fact the whole passage – cannot but recall Flaubert's vision of the pure novel, deriving all its strength from internal not external resources.

Huysmans himself, in the musings of Durtal, offered a description of what he was doing: 'Il faudrait . . . suivre la grande voie si profondément creusée par Zola, mais il serait nécessaire aussi de tracer en l'air un chemin parallèle, une autre route, d'atteindre les en deça et les après, de faire, en un mot, un naturalisme spiritualiste' [One would have to keep to the road so boldly driven through by Zola, but it would also be necessary to build a parallel road in the air, a companion route, to reach what lies beyond; to create, that is, a spiritual naturalism] (*Là-Bas*, p. 8). As we have seen, it was the word realism and not naturalism that adapted itself to this new context. But more important for the moment than the word used, more or less illegitimately, to describe its manifestations is the fact that idealism had gained the initiative in literature; that many writers would have repeated after the 'revisionist' Ernest Renan in 1890, 'pour nous autres, idéalistes, une seule doctrine est vraie, la doctrine transcendante selon laquelle le but de l'humanité est la constitution d'une conscience[1] superieure . . . ' [for those of us who are idealists, one doctrine alone is true, the transcendental doctrine according to which the goal of humanity is the establishment of a higher consciousness . . .] (*Oeuvres*, III, p. 725).

One effect of this appeal to 'une conscience supérieure' rather than to the undisturbed, normative consciousness of the ordinary waking world was the rehabilitation of dream, aspiration, intuition, and other states and faculties beyond the control and

[1] The first meaning of 'conscience' in French is 'consciousness'.

cognizance of science. In the same symptomatic preface (to the delayed *l'Avenir de la Science*) Ernest Renan said 'je ne figure pas comment on rebatira, sans les anciens rêves, les assises d'une vie noble et heureuse' [I cannot imagine how, without the time-honoured dreams, we shall rebuild the foundation of a happy and worthy life] (pp. 726–7); and Edmond de Goncourt sounds almost like the early Yeats when he confesses, in his preface to *Les Frères Zemganno* (1879), that he found himself 'en un état de l'âme ou la vérité trop vraie m'était antipathique à moi aussi! – et j'ai fait cette fois de l'imagination dans du rêve mêlé à du souvenir' [in a state of mind where truths too true didn't appeal even to me – and I have exercised my imagination this time in a mixture of dreams and memories] (p. xii).

It was surrealism that sought most consistently to release these forces. André Breton said that surrealism relied upon 'la croyance à la réalité supérieure de certains formes d'association negligées jusqu'à lui, à la toute-puissance du rêve, au jeu desintéressé de la pensée' [the belief in the superior reality of certain forms of association so far neglected, on the all-importance of the dream, on the disinterested play of mind] (*Manifestes du Surréalisme*, p. 40) and Yves Duplessis offers a summary of surrealist philosophy that brings us back to the movement away from the material, the 'dislocation of reality':

> Not only is psychology overturned by these revelations; the physical sciences are overturned too by the discovery of a world subject to discontinuity and indeterminacy. The task of literature will be to discover the unity of the individual behind the multiplicity of its aspects. Similarly in painting; movements like cubism bring about a genuine dislocation of reality and struggle to get beyond appearances to the essence of people and things.
>
> (*Le Surréalisme*, 1967, p. 9)

As Picasso is recorded as saying, 'When you come right down to it, all you have is your self. Your self is a sun with a thousand rays in your belly. The rest is nothing' (Herbert Read *A Concise History of Modern Painting*, London, 1959; p. 147).

III

The stress on the individual experience, the individual vision, became more and more emphatic until it reached its terminal form in surrealism; and one may see in this gravitation towards subjectivity the most obvious characteristic of idealism in literature. Zola had written in *Mes Haines* (1866) that 'une oeuvre d'art est un coin de la création vu à travers un tempérament' [a work of art is a corner of creation seen through a temperament] (p. 25), and what happened was that the thing seen receded and the act of seeing advanced in relative importance. The new dispensation is defended with vigour by Maupassant in his essay 'Le Roman', prefixed to his novel *Pierre et Jean* (1888), where he rejects the childishness of naïve realism:

> Quel enfantillage, d'ailleurs, de croire à la réalité puisque nous portons chacun la nôtre dans notre pensée et dans nos organes. Nos yeux, nos oreilles, notre odorat, notre gout differents créent autant de vérités qu'il y a hommes sur la terre ... Chacun de nous se fait donc simplement une illusion du monde ... Et l'écrivain n'a autre mission que de reproduire fidèlement cette illusion avec tous les procédés d'art q'uil a appris et dont il peut disposer ... les grands artistes sont ceux qui imposent à l'humanité leur illusion particuliére'.

> [How childish it is, anyway, to rely on reality when each of us carries his own in his mind and body. Our eyes, our ears, our sense of smell, our taste, all different, create as many realities as there are people on the earth ... So every one of us simply creates his own illusion of the world ... And the writer has no other task but to reproduce faithfully this illusion with all the art he is master of and which will be of use to him ... The great artists are those who force us to accept their own illusion.]

> (*Oeuvres*, XIX, pp. xv–xvi)

Objective reality has become fragmented, dispersed among a limitless number of conflicting subjectivities; it is no longer a solid substance, but the sum of our illusions – and it is the more plausible illusion that earns the description of reality. René Wellek comments that 'the accepted nineteenth century meaning of realism is turned upside down' when this readjustment is complete, when a critic can claim that the internal stream-of-consciousness is the only realistic method and therefore '"the subjective experience . . . is the only objective experience".' (*Concepts of Criticism*, p. 237).

Stephen Dedalus 'drew less pleasure from the reflection of the glowing sensible world through the prism of a language many-coloured and richly storied than from the contemplation of an inner world of individual emotions mirrored perfectly in a lucid supple periodic prose' (*Portrait*, p. 176), and Lawrence's confident gradation and distribution of reality proceeds from his automatic rejection of 'the superficial unreal world of fact' (*Women in Love*, p. 438). Samuel Beckett explains how 'the artist is active, but negatively, shrinking from the nullity of extracircumferential phenomena, drawn in to the core of the eddy', and endorses Proust's exposure of 'the grotesque fallacy of a realistic art', his 'contempt for the literature that "describes", for the realists and naturalists worshipping the offal of experience'. It is much in the style of James that Beckett goes on to locate the subjective experience at the centre of the artist's work: 'the only possible hierarchy in the world of objective phenomena is represented by a table of their respective coefficients of penetration, that is to say, in the terms of the subject (Another sneer at the realists)' (*Proust and 3 dialogues with Georges Duthuit*, London, 1968, pp. 65–6, 76, 78, 84).

It was in James's prefaces that the novel became for the first time fully conscious, woke to a sharpened sense of its own possibilities. Persistently James displays his belief that what we call reality is a personal refraction, an involuntary 'point of view' that may be compared to the voluntary 'point of view' the artist adopts in his delineation of life. This is how James's narrative tends to become 'not . . . my own impersonal account of the affair in hand, but . . . my account of somebody's impression of it' (*AN*, p. 327):

> the figures in any picture, the agents in any drama, are interesting only in proportion as they feel their respective situations . . . Their being finely aware – as Hamlet and Lear, say, are finely aware – *makes* absolutely the intensity of their adventure, gives the maximum of intensity to what befalls them.
>
> (*AN*, p. 62)

The stuff of experience is nothing except as led into the arena of significance by a responsive consciousness; the goings-on of life itself are uninteresting, a 'dull waste', unless redeemed by a mind alert to its reverberations. And so James's characters have to be 'intense *perceivers*, all, of their respective predicaments', this perception being that which then creates or 'makes absolutely' the situation in which they find themselves. James says of Newman (from *The American*) that 'the interest of everything is all that it is *his* vision, *his* conception, *his* interpretation . . . He therefore supremely matters; all the rest matters only as he feels it, treats it, meets it' (*AN*, p. 37). James creates his 'light vessel of consciousness' (*AN*, p. 143), and then discovers reality in terms of its operations; the real – the 'transmuted real' – being 'the fruit of a process that adds to observation what a kiss adds to a greeting' (*Partial Portraits*, p. 217).

Like Stephen Dedalus, all James's central characters are 'drawn forth to go to encounter reality'. But James is more scrupulous in his use of the words real, reality, realism than earlier theorists of the novel, as one can see from his dramatization of the problem of determining the real in his short story 'The Real Thing'. He prefers to use the word intensity. Intensity is what the novelist must strive for: 'Without intensity where is vividness, and without vividness where is presentability?' (*AN*, p. 66); intensity gives in itself the 'communicated closeness of truth' (*AN*, p. 255), it *is* the 'force interne' Flaubert spoke of; it is intensity that qualifies the reality as real. But he does offer a definition of realism as 'the real most finely mixed with life, which *is* in the last analysis the ideal' (*Notes on Novelists*, p. 396); and this usage clearly explains how the word rode the reaction against materialism. Realism surrendered the 'thing' at its centre – or let it become completely overlaid – and attached itself with great flexibility to any conception of reality. If, as Blake maintained, 'every thing possible to be believ'd is an image of truth', then realism may be used to describe the figuring-forth of that truth, whatever it should be.

And this is the justification for my division of realism into two different, almost contradictory, postures of meaning. Because the 'realism' intended by Yeats when he writes of Blake's 'visionary realism', or required by Harry Levin in appealing to 'the romantic realism of Dickens, the "fantastic" realism of Dostoevsky, and the "poetic" realism of Otto Ludwig' (see above, p. 1) has emancipated itself from its simple scrupulous conscience: it has become *conscious* (if I may speak of the word as 'aware' of its own meaning), it has understood the new situation and adapted itself accordingly. This extended sense of the word certainly trespasses beyond the bounds envisaged by Duranty; for him, the word would seem to have degenerated from its pristine purity of the 1850s. '*Réalisme* est mort, vive le Réalisme,' he proclaimed in the last number of his journal; but he could scarcely have anticipated the curious reincarnations that were to follow. An obvious incitement to these successive metamorphoses lies in what we have before alluded to, the word's equivocal status. Realism is not only vague and elastic, but also pretentious in the implicit claim it makes to determine reality. No apologist for his own vision will tamely let the 'real' be appropriated by some other; and so it is forced into new postures, encouraged in new pretences, until everyone has his different claim upon it. This is the situation we are in now, with competing critics pulling the word a dozen different ways; and one can only make sense of it by the kind of disentanglement I am attempting here in miniature.

IV

Conscious realism I use to describe the result of what might be seen as a new contract established between the writer and reality. This new contract is best summarized in the sentence Yeats used when he tried 'to put all into a phrase' in the last letter he wrote: 'Man can embody truth but he cannot know it' (*Letters*, p. 922). Reality is not knowable – it may not be 'corresponded to', imitated, mocked, understood: such a notion is an impossible crudity. If aggressively pursued, reality recedes; only when invoked will it advance, and manifest itself ideally, in essence, rather than in the 'inclusion and confusion' of its (in any case unrepeatable) existence. Man embodies truth in art: which is therefore a kind of 'knowing', not an abstract or scientific knowing but an act, an affirmation; the kind of knowing that expresses itself not in description, repetition, or imitation, but in making, making new: 'The world knows nothing because it has made nothing, we know everything because we have made everything' (*Selected Criticism*, ed. Jeffares, London, 1965, p. 256).

It is in this view that the poet – the writer in his most general sense of 'maker' – becomes a 'demi-urge'; a sharer in the labour of creation. This is the central belief of symbolism, and there are many well-known statements of it that one may use as illustration. Many of these, naturally, ante-date symbolism itself, as many of the realist ideas were in circulation before 1850. Especially when it is considered beside the uncompromising literalness of Plato in *The Republic*, Longinus's *On the Sublime* already suggests what might loosely be called symbolist ideas; as when he says of the oratory of

E

Hyperides that 'we are attracted away from the demonstration of
fact to the startling image' (trans. T. S. Dorsch; Penguin ed.,
p. 124). But certainly the most interesting of early accounts – itself
'startling', even – is that given by Sidney in his *Apology for Poetry*.
Sidney contrasts the poetic with all other activities precisely in its
being a making. 'There is no art delivered to mankind that hath
not the works of Nature for his principal object, without which
they could not consist, and on which they so depend, as they
become actors and players, as it were, of what Nature will have set
forth.' Thus for the astronomer, the musician, the natural philosopher (or naturalist), the lawyer, the historian, the physician:
they serve a pre-existing reality, they defer to the fact.

> Only the poet, disdaining to be tied to any such subjection, lifted up
> with the vigour of his own invention, doth grow in effect another
> nature, in making things either better than Nature bringeth forth, or,
> quite anew, forms such as never were in Nature, as the Heroes,
> Demigods, Cyclops, Chimeras, Furies, and such like: so as he goeth
> hand in hand with Nature, not enclosed within the narrow warrant of
> her gifts, but freely ranging only within the zodiac of his own wit.
> (*English Critical Essays*, 16th–18th centuries, ed. E. D. Jones, Lon-
> don, 1958, pp. 6–7)

There is little one can add to this. When Wallace Stevens says that
'the poem is a nature created by the poet' (*OP*, p. 166) he is simply
making an abrupt précis of Sidney's persuasive argument.

But other writers have had their versions, each of which provides evidence for the creative power of the imagination, the
'shaping spirit', and offers an abbreviated account of its operation.
Fielding defended the mythologizing of the classical poets (against
his own prejudice) by suggesting that 'they are not, indeed, so
properly said to turn reality into fiction, as fiction into reality'
(preface to *A Voyage to Lisbon*; Everyman ed., p. 86). The meaning
of fiction as something *made* is clearly necessary here. 'I am certain
of nothing but of the holiness of the Heart's affections and the

truth of Imagination – what the imagination seizes as Beauty must be truth – whether it existed before or not,' wrote Keats to Bailey (22 Nov. 1817). The last phrase throws into deliberate relief Keats's faith in the generative power of the individual vision: truth may be made not found, made (as diamond is made, out of inferior elements) by intensity of perception, that pressure that gathers in the mind, like gravity, and urges it towards the certain core of truth. Keats proceeds with an illuminating image: 'the Imagination may be compared to Adam's dream – he awoke and found it truth'. This is an inclusive concept of truth ('everything possible to be believed . . . ', again), in which everything may be true, except that which unseasonably asserts itself to be so, tries to establish itself with an 'irritable reaching after fact and reason' (Keats: letter to his brothers, 22 Dec. 1817) and forfeits the generous allowance of the imagination. 'But the poet,' said Sidney, 'never affirmeth. The poet never maketh any circles about your imagination, to conjure you to believe for true what he writes . . . ' (p. 33). The appeal to the inferior, demonstrable truth is a distraction, a self-injury; it is the writer asking to have himself taken at a lower valuation. James says that the historical novelist needs to lay down his burden of facts to achieve 'a superior harmony which shall be after all a superior truth' (*Notes on Novelists*, p. 394).

We might return to James for his account of the writer's 'independent world in which nothing is right save as we rightly imagine it' (*AN*, p. 171), where 'we move through a blest world in which we know nothing except by style, but in which also everything is saved by it, and in which the image is thus always superior to the thing itself'; where 'art makes life', where 'expression is creation and makes the reality' (*Letters*, II, 490; *Notes on Novelists*, p. 100); but space will hardly permit such self-indulgence. 'Where man is not, nature is barren' (Blake); for the writer of symbolist temper, where consciousness is not, reality is uncreated, lies hidden from the light of the mind like the dark side of the moon.

Critics of similar persuasion have been eager to endorse this view of the poem as a contribution to reality: in some sense itself a thing. According to Ortega y Gasset, 'the poet aggrandizes the world by adding to reality, which is there by itself, the continents of his imagination. Author derives from *auctor*, he who augments' (*The Dehumanization of Art*, p. 31). Santayana criticizes the habitual use of the word 'expression' at all, because of a mistaken idea inseparable from its use as a metaphor to describe utterance: 'expression is a misleading term which suggests that something previously known is rendered or imitated; whereas the expression is itself an original fact, the values of which are then referred to the thing expressed, much as the honours of a Chinese mandarin are attributed retroactively to his parents' (*Selected Critical Writings*, 1968, vol. I, p. 74).

The painter Mondrian was led by the developing austerity of his theory and technique to formulate a position which resembles and reinforces this. 'According to Mondrian,' writes Frank Elgar, 'the modern painter must turn completely away from nature and seek inspiration in his own mind. He must cease to offer an image of the exterior world or the illusion of sensory reality; he must substitute a new, autonomous reality which is valid both in itself and by itself' (*Mondrian*, London, 1968, p. 110). One can think of Mondrian as a Beckett of art, 'shrinking,' as he likewise did, 'from the nullity of extracircumferential phenomena', and constructing 'a more real existence' for his paintings by restraining them within the two-dimensional world they properly inhabit. And remaining for a moment with criticism of the visual arts, one finds a satisfying phrase used by Harold Osborne to describe Topolski's drawings: 'their aim is ... the creation of an emergent reality which stands on its own feet and is justified not by what it represents but by what it itself is and what it offers for appreciation' ('The Use of Nature in Art,' *British Journal of Aesthetics* II (1962), p. 326). The argument is the same; and this description of the reality of art as 'emergent' contains in a word the idea I am trying to illustrate in this chapter.

V

One has to insist that what I call conscious realism is not a simple reaction against the earlier realism, chained as this was to the oar of the material world. The situation is more complex: the conscious realist does not reject the world (except when provoked, and then only as part of his strategy); he maintains he has achieved a subtler and more satisfactory synthesis between those crude abstractions reality and imagination, and those equally crude adjustable spanners of criticism, objective and subjective. Flaubert said that reality for him was only a 'tremplin' or springboard, and wrote to another correspondent: 'Croyez-vous donc que cette ignoble realité, dont la reproduction vous dégoûte, ne me fasse tout autant qu'à vous sauter le coeur? Si vous me connaissiez davantage, vous sauriez que j'ai la vie ordinaire en exécration' [Don't you think that this unworthy reality, whose reproduction disgusts you, doesn't turn my stomach also? If you knew me better, you would know that I execrate ordinary life]. His last novel *Bouvard et Pécuchet* is the articulation of this disgust, in its ridicule of the positivist ideal, as his two mindless heroes seek – like Beckett's Watt – to know and name their world. But a springboard is after all a necessity; and Flaubert elsewhere stipulated that 'il faut que la réalité extérieure entre en nous, à nous en faire presque crier, pour la bien reproduire' [exterior reality must enter into us, must make us almost cry out, if we are to reproduce it well]. He even confessed to Louise Colet that he had 'two distinct personalities' as a writer: 'un qui est épris de *gueulades*, de lyrisme, de grands vols d'aigle, de toutes les sonorités de la phrase et des sommets de l'idée; un autre qui fouille et creuse le vrai tant qu'il peut, qui aime à accuser le petit fait aussi puissamment que le grand, qui voudrait vous faire sentir, presque *matériellement* les choses qu'il reproduit . . .' [one who is fascinated by bombast, lyricism, great eagle flights, all the sonorities of style and the high summits of ideas; another who burrows and digs for the truth as far as he can, who likes to give the small detail as much emphasis as the significant fact, who wants you to feel the things he represents with an almost physical immediacy . . .] (*Correspondance*, VII, p. 350; IV, p. 125; III, p. 269; II, pp. 343–4). Émile Faguet summarized this duality well when he said of Flaubert that 'the imagination was his muse and reality his conscience' (*Flaubert*, 1899, p. 66). It is in the preface to *The American* that James takes up this question of the apparent alternatives of subjective and objective, romantic and realistic, and subjects them to a scrutiny which leads him to reject the idea of their *being* alternatives: 'it is as difficult . . . to trace the dividing-line between the real and the romantic as to plant a milestone between north and south' (*AN*, p. 37). He describes first how the originating idea for the novel 'promptly put on . . . the objectivity it had wanted', but that in the working out 'my conception unfurled, with the best conscience in the world, the emblazoned flag of romance' (*AN*, pp. 23, 25). James then puts the question of when and how the aims of the romantic and realistic artists declare themselves as radically different from each other. This it is not easy to answer; and he goes on in fact to suggest that in any writer worth talking about, no simple division is possible between the two tendencies: 'the interest is greatest . . . when he commits himself in both directions; not quite at the same time or to the same effect, of course, but by some need of performing his whole possible revolution, by the law of some rich passion in him for extremes' (*AN*, p. 31).

It is certainly evidence of intellectual if not necessarily of artistic progress that when idealism regained the initiative in the 1890s it did not try to outlaw some higher synthesis which should make the 'passion for extremes' indeed a *rich* passion, and not merely something destructive. Civilization would not advance if each new culture razed to the ground all evidence of earlier cultures; nor does literature stand to gain much from the kind of polemic that went on in France around 1850 in the name of realism. But later in the century the spirit of truth seemed, for once, more effective than the spirit of faction; and a review by William Sharp of a Howells novel in *The Academy* for 1890 offers a good example of the patient understanding that was replacing the earlier bland assertions:

> Perhaps realism in literary art may be approximately defined as the science of exact presentment of many complexities, abstract and concrete, in one truthful, because absolutely reasonable and apparently inevitable, synthesis; this, *plus* the creative energy which in high development involves what is misleadingly called the romantic spirit, and *minus* that weakness of the selective faculty which is the dominant factor in the work of the so-called realists of the Zolaesque school. Thus regarded, realism and romance are found to be as indissoluble as soul and body in a living human being. The true artist, no doubt, is he who is neither a realist nor a romanticist, but in whose work is observable the shaping power of the higher qualities of the methods of genuine realism and the higher qualities of the methods of genuine romance.
>
> (in *ECN*, p. 56)

The 'shaping spirit of Imagination' and the 'shaping strength' of science are fortuitously combined in Sharp's 'shaping power', which shall include them both. The writer starts with things; but it is not enough for him simply to 'name' these. The details must somehow be made active, available. 'Reality is a cliché from which we escape by metaphor' (Stevens; *OP*, p. 179): it is metaphor, working like a germ of energy among the 'facts', that makes them so, adds what one might call the yeast of the imagination to the material dough. Proust describes the process in *Le Temps Retrouvé* – the process that establishes reality itself.

Ce que nous appelons la réalité est un certain rapport entre ces sensations et ces souvenirs qui nous entourent simultanément – rapport que
supprime une simple vision cinématographique, laquelle s'éloigne par
là d'autant plus vrai qu'elle prétend se borner à lui – rapport unique
que l'écrivain doit retrouver pour en enchaîner à jamais dans sa
phrase les deux termes différents. On peut faire se succéder indéfini-
ment dans une description les objets qui figuraient dans le lieu décrit,
la vérité ne commencera qu'au moment où l'écrivain prendra deux
objets différents, posera leur rapport, analogue dans le monde de
l'art à celui qu'est le rapport unique de la loi causale dans le monde de
la science, et les enfermera dans les anneaux nécessaires d'un beau
style; même, ainsi que la vie, quant, en rapprochant une qualité commune à deux sensations, il dégagera leur essence commune en les
réunissant l'une et l'autre pour les soustraire aux contingences du
temps, dans une métaphore.

[What we call reality is a certain relation between these sensations
and these memories which surround us simultaneously – a relation
which is destroyed by a simple cinematographic vision, which loses
hold of the real by its very submission to it – an unique relation which
the writer must recover to bind the two terms eternally together in
his words. He may describe things from the original situation one
after another, but the truth will only declare itself when the writer
takes two different objects and establishes their relationship, a
parallel in the world of art to the unique relation of causality in the
world of science, and delays them in the requisite toils of style; or, as
in life, when drawing together a quality common to two sensations,
he will extract their essence, detaching them from the contingencies
of time, and unite them in metaphor.]

(Livre de Poche ed., Paris, 1967, pp. 248–9)

Metaphor conciliates two worlds; if the theorist wishes to endorse
this conciliation, then the word realism has to be stretched to
accommodate the new design. We come as close as we can to the
actual moment of growth – when realism puts forth new shoots –
in Hector Agosti's 'Defensa del Realismo' of 1944: 'the constant
interpenetration of the individual and the collectivity is an attri-

bute of this dynamic realism, for which we need to find another name. Since it is neither ignominiously objective nor extravagantly subjective, I would suggest, rather than dynamic, that we call it *super-subjective*' (trans. Becker; *DMLR*, p. 497).

The positive effect of this conciliation is to liberate the word realism from the restrictive interpretation of the early realists, with their materialist philosophy and their reductive aesthetic and technique. It enables Meredith to say that 'between realism and idealism there is no natural conflict' (cit. R. G. Davis, 'The Sense of the Real in English Fiction', *Comparative Literature*, III (1951), p. 215). The negative effect is to deprive it of any meaning whatsoever. Burke said that freedom must be limited in order to be possessed; and the same applies to meaning as it is possessed by words. It remains a question of whether the word realism can make use of its freedom; whether it can crystallize these new elements, and limit its meaning in a new usefulness.

4
Conclusion

The exploration of realism is, as Harry Levin admits, ultimately subsumed in the larger question of the relationship between life and art (*GH*, p. 3). But one need not abandon all hope of particularizing the argument – restraining it within the harbour of manageable ideas rather than letting it drift out (as Fielding said the disorderly novel did) on 'the opening of wilds or seas'. One may restrain it with the fundamental question of representation; and with questions involving the relation of this representation to its subject.

The naïve realist, we have seen, imagines that the world is susceptible of re-presentation in words, or in some other medium, and that he may achieve this re-presentation by professing to do so, and committing himself to the task with simplicity and sincerity. With this simple confidence Zola can argue that 'le premier caractère du Roman naturaliste . . . est la reproduction exacte de la vie' [the leading characteristic of the naturalist novel . . . is the exact reproduction of life] (*RN*, p. 22). But it may easily be shown that 'representation' is not only a technical but also a philosophical impossibility; at best an inaccurate metaphor (like expression) and at worst a troublesome source of confused thinking.

The mirror has always provided the best image for the representation theory; Stendhal saw the novel as a mirror travelling along a highway. But the limitations of this image are unwittingly exposed by Edmund Gosse in his article 'The Limits of Realism in Fiction' (1890), when he writes of 'the inherent disproportion which exists between the small flat surface of a book and the vast arch of life which it undertakes to mirror' (in *DMLR*, p. 390). The surface of a book, be it small or large, cannot usefully be thought of as a mirror; it is not a matter of 'disproportion' between life and book, but of different modes of being, to whose subtle relation the simple image of reflection is manifestly inadequate.

The limiting effect of the 'mirror' image is most obvious in the visual arts, and it was in the rebellion of painters against the pointless, endless labour of representation – well documented in Herbert Read's *A Concise History of Modern Painting* (1959) – that provided some of the most damaging arguments against it. Read believes modern painting to be unified by 'the intention, as Klee said, not to reflect the visible, but to make visible' (p. 8). He describes Kandinsky's treatise *Über das Geistige in der Kunst* (1912; translated as *Concerning the Spiritual in Art*, 1914) as 'the first tentative justification of non-objective art': the analogies which Kandinsky draws with music are intended to stress the formal rather than the contentual element in art, and there is also a significant emphasis on technique. 'An expression of a slowly formed inner feeling, worked over repeatedly and almost pedantically. This I call a *Composition*. In this reason, consciousness, purpose play an overwhelming part.' (Read, pp. 170, 172.) Klee used the image of a tree, simply and effectively, in his lecture *Über die moderne Kunst* (1924; translated as *On Modern Art*, London, 1948) to defend the artist's emancipation from a superficially conceived mimesis.

Nobody will expect a tree to form its crown in exactly the same way as its root. Between above and below there cannot be exact mirror images of each other. It is obvious that different functions operating in different elements must produce vital divergencies. But it is just the artist who at times is denied those departures from nature which his art demands. He has even been accused of incompetence and deliberate distortion.

(Read, p. 183)

We have already seen how Mondrian came to realize that the painter 'must turn completely away from nature'; 'why', he argues again, 'should art continue to follow nature, when every other field has left nature behind?' (Elgar, *Mondrian*, pp. 110–11).

Many modern theorists have insisted on the bankruptcy of the representational theory in literature also. R. G. Collingwood argues this out in his chapter 'Art and Representation' in his *The Principles of Art* (London, 1938), from the position that 'today, the only tolerable view is that no art is representative' (p. 43). Ortega y Gasset derides the assumption that 'the author can do nothing but copy reality. So coarse a reasoning lies at the bottom of what is currently called "realism" ' (*The Dehumanization of Art*, p. 102). Susanne Langer prefers the term 'transformation' to 'imitation': this 'consists in the rendering of a desired appearance without any actual representation of it, by the production of an equivalent sense-impression rather than a literally similar one, in terms of the limited, legitimate material which cannot naïvely copy the desired property of the original' (*Problems of Art*, London, 1957, p. 98). And Winifred Nowottny follows up a similar observation – 'the nature of language is such that there can be no such thing as a neutral transcription of an object into words' – with a direct reference to realism as most obviously dependent on this mistaken idea (*The Language Poets Use*, London, 1962, p. 45).

It is not far from maintaining the literal idea of representation to proposing the false objective of substitution: where the representation shall be so perfect as to be mistaken for the 'real thing'. Arthur McDowall reminds us of the triviality of this 'trompe l'oeil' design, in its muddling confusion of categories: '*Trompe-l'oeil* is life in the wrong place, and can scarcely be called art. It is the custom to call it realism, and it does represent a realistic misconception or extreme; it is the Nemesis which waits for a realism that has forgotten the conditions of art' (*Realism*, p. 40). A specious argument tends to develop about the relative value of the representation and the thing represented; an argument as to which is 'more real'. This has its source, no doubt, in Plato, with the hierarchy of realities outlined in *The Republic*: first, the essential reality of the idea, then the manufactured reality of created things, and last of all the imitated reality of art. But Plato had a metaphysic to justify his discrimination; the idea as we encounter it in modern times is more often a result of simple carelessness. We find the materialist Chernishevsky for example saying, 'such then is the purpose of art – it does not improve reality, does not beautify it, it reproduces it, serves as its substitute' (in *DMLR*, p. 64). The succession is easy from seeing art as 'la reproduction exacte de la vie' to seeing it, as here, as its substitute, and eventually its competitor: as if the two must be thought of as alternatives, straining against each other in some kind of ontological tug-of-war.

This curious idea survives in more sophisticated discussion. André Malraux says in *Les Voix du Silence* (1951) that 'les grands artistes ne sont pas les transcripteurs du monde, ils en sont les rivaux' (p. 451). And Gide lets his novelist character Édouard in *Les Faux Monnayeurs* realize the basic theme of his own novel in these terms: 'ce sera sans doute la rivalité du monde réel et de la representation que nous en faisons' (Livre de Poche ed., p. 255). Erich Heller concludes his article 'The Realistic Fallacy' by saying that 'the economy of the world cannot support forever the expensive households of so many creators competing with creation itself' (*DMLR*, p. 598). It is the idea of competition that is out of place. Ortega prefers to see it as a matter of collaboration, where the artist 'aggrandizes the world by adding to reality'. This does not mean that he duplicates what is already there – Kenneth Graham suggests that for many nineteenth-century critics, ' "realism" of characterization resulted almost literally in an addition to the country's population' (*ECN*, p. 23) – but that he 'bringeth his own stuff' to stimulate the dialectical process by which the mind carries on its critique of reality, its realization of the potentially real.

It is the symbolist writers who have usually been accused of disparaging life, and setting up art in competition with it. The evidence for this charge is not hard to find, from writers like Gautier – generally regarded, from his preface to *Mademoiselle de Maupin* (1835) as founder of the art for art's sake school – the decadent Huysmans, and Villiers-de-l'Isle-Adam, whose character Axel (quintessence of Poe's aesthetic recluses) provides the most dramatic example by relegating the business of living to the servants' quarters. But this evidence is not so conclusive as it might seem. The essential thing in symbolist theory is not its relative valuation of life and art (which is part of a rhetorical structure) but its sane assertion of their separate categories. So when Gautier writes 'No, you fools . . . you can't make soup from a book; a novel isn't a pair of seamless boots; a sonnet isn't a syringe; a play isn't a railway', he isn't so much disparaging the benefits of contemporary technology as reminding his audience that science and art answer different needs. And even when he goes on, more provocatively, 'I humbly confess that I would rather have my shoe come unstitched than my lines clumsily rhymed, and I could do without boots rather than poems' (Garnier-Flammarion ed., pp. 42, 44), Gautier is in fact ridiculing the idea of shoes and poetry being considered as alternatives, exposing the absurdity of weighing the world of matter against the world of mind.

The writer who accepts the implications of consciousness knows he must break from the close embrace of life if there is to be any art at all, any statement which shall survive its context. 'Mêlé à la vie, on la voit mal' wrote Flaubert to his mother (*Correspondance*, II, p. 269), and James observed that 'one has a horror . . . artistically, of agitated reflexions' (*AN*, p. 27). Wilde's character Vivian in the *Decay of Lying* dialogue regards life as 'the solvent that breaks up Art, the enemy that lays waste her house'. The writer in these cases leaves himself open to the charge that he is rejecting life. But what he is really rejecting is contaminated art, art deprived of its own privileges, art made tongue-tied by the authority of 'common-sense', positivist and righteous realism. And so the abuse is misdirected; life suffers no disparagement. In fact it is easy to see that all assertions of the value of art must be taken up, ultimately, in the value of life, which is the larger term: the formal antithesis is (as I have said) a rhetorical device, designed to protect art – in the interests of life – from the unreasonable bullying of life itself, impatient for its golden eggs.

Paradoxically, it is the realist, with the cry of 'life' upon his lips, who really offers the disparagement: disparaging life by claiming it may be reproduced, disparaging art by claiming it is a reproduction, disparaging both by seeing them in the wrong relation to each other. 'Most modern reproducers of life,' says Stevens, 'even including the camera, really repudiate it'; it is in this light that 'realism is a corruption of reality' (*OP*, pp. 176, 166).

II

The sanest position, then, would seem to be one that admits the separate categories of art and life and accounts for the relationship between them, and the kind of 'realism' attainable in achieving this relationship, with a conscious and deliberate awareness of the possibilities and impossibilities involved. In his book *Time and the Novel* A. A. Mendilow describes how literature 'first tries to reflect reality as faithfully and as fully as it can, and then, despairing of the attempt, tries to evoke the feeling of a new reality of its own' (p. 39). The artist has to live in the kingdom created out of this despair: like a fallen angel, he must admit to himself the impracticability of seeking to re-enter heaven, trying to live again by conscience and obedience alone. Better to reign in Hell than serve in Heaven: he is come to consciousness, and must accept the penalties and privileges of his new state. Art is an effect of the impurity of man's condition, if one likes of his fallen nature, where primal innocence is destroyed by self-knowledge, and peace given over to the aspirations and dissatisfactions of the reflective consciousness. 'The act of self-consciousness is for *us* the source and principle of all *our* possible knowledge' (Coleridge, *Biographia Literaria*; ch. 12: thesis X). It is therefore unreasonable to expect of the artist that he should become somehow unconscious, revert to a state of single innocence; but the objectives of naïve realism could certainly be interpreted in this way. Walter Ong has described, in a brilliant short essay, how metaphor offers a kind of satisfaction to this intellectual nostalgia for a pre-dualistic stage of consciousness ('Metaphor and the Twinned Vision', *The Barbarian Within*, New York, 1962, pp. 41–8); but the puritanical realist – and the *nouveau romancier* – rejects metaphor as a contrivance in his obstinate burrowing away from the light of the mind.

So whereas the realism of conscience derived all its strength from its simplicity, realism in its conscious phase depends upon an awareness of its own complexity. Wallace Stevens has another fine aphorism among his 'Adagia': 'The final belief is to believe in a fiction, which you know to be a fiction, there being nothing else. The exquisite truth is to know that it is a fiction and that you believe in it willingly' (*OP*, p. 163). As Coleridge indicated in his formula 'the willing suspension of disbelief', it is the *willingness* of the belief that makes all the difference: the difference between a simple belief, which has been encouraged to ignore all the problems, and a 'final belief', which has been deliberately led through them and informed by them; between a crude truth which lies readily to hand, and may be wielded with any sudden slogan, and an 'exquisite truth' which is the result of an enlightened complicity between the writer and the reader.

If the writer invites his reader's consciousness of the conditions of his work – as Sterne does in *Tristram Shandy*, seeking almost to involve the reader in the very process of writing itself: one thinks of his appeal for the reader's assistance in getting Uncle Toby to move off the stairs – it is only as a result of his exercising his own unremittingly upon it. Nothing happens by accident: there is no question of a book's 'writing itself'. Champfleury maintained he had written many stories without knowing what he was doing (*Le Réalisme*, p. 6); how far removed is this from James, who deliberated over every 'humblest question' in the writing of his novels, 'even to that of the shade of a cadence or the position of a comma' (*AN*, p. 345). The naïve realist, guided by the light of his conscience, tries to ignore the actual process of creation as far as possible: one senses almost a distaste at the thought of sitting at a desk *writing*. But the informed realist knows he is guided only by the light of his mind, and so the process itself assumes a great importance – a greater importance, it sometimes seemed to James, than the eventual result:

> There is the story of one's hero, and then, thanks to the intimate connexion of things, the story of one's story itself. I blush to confess it, but if one's a dramatist one's a dramatist, and the later imbroglio is liable on occasion to strike me as really the more objective of the two.
>
> (*AN*, p. 313)

It is no irreverence, then, for James to speak of 'the game of art' and refer to the 'fun' of composition, although F. R. Leavis would certainly see such attitudes as evidence of James's 'disproportionate interest in technique' (*The Great Tradition*; Peregrine ed., Harmondsworth, 1962, p. 188). It conduces to the 'final belief', the 'exquisite truth', that James should dwell on 'the inveterate romance of the labour' (*AN*, p. 287) in this way. It is a matter, again, of sanely considering the possibilities of art collaterally with the possibilities of life. 'Really, universally, relations stop nowhere, and the exquisite problem of the artist is eternally but to draw, by a geometry of his own, the circle within which they shall happily *appear* to do so' (*AN*, p. 5). Our consciousness of the 'exquisite problem' and our delight in its resolution, is an additional incentive to a belief which may be seen as 'springing not from an artless and measureless, but from a conscious and cultivated credulity' (*AN*, p. 171); which realizes and willingly accepts that the reality acceded to is a fiction: a reality which has been made, rather than another which has been corrupted by representation. In Robert Scholes's formula, we need to accept 'the artificiality of the real and the reality of the artificial' (*The Fabulators*, p. 20).

III

Although one recognizes that such a sophistication has scarcely affected general usage – which still intends by realism the close rendering of ordinary experience – one must conclude that on the theoretical front, on the drawing-boards of criticism, the meaning of realism has become generalized to include the achievement of reality, the creation of belief, however this may be arrived at.

The tendency to derestrict the attribution of realism may be observed already in the nineteenth century, as we have seen above; but with more modern theorists it becomes the only possible development. Harry Levin takes advantage of an 'enlarged perspective' to claim that 'all great writers, in so far as they are committed to a searching and scrupulous critique of life as they know it, may be reckoned among the realists' (*GH*, p. 83). And Arthur McDowall goes even further towards a relativistic conclusion, dropping all 'qualifications' for realism: naturalism insists that art 'should be cut to a certain pattern, while realism is, or should be, prepared for all its possible manifestations'. Realism becomes nothing more (and nothing less) than 'the *sine qua non* of artistic significance' (*Realism*, pp. 24, 50). But perhaps the most conclusive evidence of the need to adopt a relativistic attitude is provided inadvertently by Erich Auerbach in his *Mimesis* (1946;

trans. 1953). Auerbach's object in this classic study of 'The Representation of Reality in Western Literature' was to assert the superiority, for the purposes of such representation, of the realistic techniques fleetingly anticipated in earlier literature but which found their full expression in nineteenth-century France. 'In so far as the serious realism of modern times cannot represent man otherwise than as embedded in a total reality, political, social, and economic, which is concrete and constantly evolving ... Stendhal is its founder' (p. 408). But because of the very scope of his work – his own 'enlarged perspective' – Auerbach exposes the insufficiency of this definition. His thesis is first shaken by 'the astounding paradox of what is called Dante's realism', 'realism projected into a changeless eternity' which 'differs from what appears and occurs on earth, yet is evidently connected with it in a necessary and strictly determined relation' (pp. 166, 169, 167). The allowance of different terms of relation is what cracks open the mould. Then Shakespeare presents problems: 'he embraces reality but he transcends it ... in a characteristically concrete but only erratically realistic manner'; 'the wealth of stylistic levels contained in Shakespeare's tragedy goes beyond actual realism' (pp. 288, 290). So much the worse for 'actual realism', one is tempted to reply, if it has to be defined by what it cannot contain. It is perhaps even more significant that Virginia Woolf, too, proves indigestible: *To the Lighthouse* 'verges upon a realm beyond reality', in it 'we are dealing with attempts to fathom a more genuine, a deeper, and indeed a more real reality' (pp. 469, 477). When Auerbach uses phrases like 'beyond reality' and 'a more real reality' he is coming up against the difficulty I described in the first chapter, that of positing a reality to which a realistic representation shall correspond. The only way of avoiding this difficulty is by avoiding the notion of correspondence, and regarding the coherence and reality of the work itself as the true criterion of realism. Auerbach has actually allowed this in respect of Homer: 'The oft-repeated reproach that Homer is a liar takes nothing from his effectiveness, he does not need to base his story on historical reality, his reality is powerful enough in itself; it ensnares us, weaving its web around us, and that suffices him. And this "real" world into which we are lured exists for itself, contains nothing but itself . . . ' (p. 11).

Admittedly this detaches the word from its historical context – asks it, indeed, to become a new word – but this is the only way to redeem it from its equivocal status to some kind of general usefulness. We may still remain conscious of the historical pretensions of realism, the 'closed shop' phase; indeed we must do so. René Wellek's article on the concept of realism, for example, is basically historicist, and he writes of realism therefore as a method, 'one method, one great stream which has its marked limitations, shortcomings, and conventions.' But he cannot avoid a critical conclusion: 'in spite of its claim to penetrate directly to life and reality, realism, in practice, has its set conventions, devices, and exclusions . . . the theory of realism is ultimately bad aesthetics because all art is "making" and is a world in itself of illusion and symbolic forms' (*Concepts of Criticism*, pp. 254–5).

One is left with a paradoxical situation. The theory of realism has been discredited; and Robert Scholes writes of those who 'continue to write frantically' in the realist-naturalist tradition as 'headless chickens unaware of the decapitating axe' (*The Fabulators*, p. 21). The word has been variously redefined by a new theoretical initiative, which sees it as representing 'the *sine qua non* of literary significance'. But it is still the old definition that governs the word in common usage (on the jackets of novels, and in the weekly journals) unperturbed by the collapse of the theoretical understructure. Perhaps this is not, after all, a paradox, but a witness to the inevitable gap between the best that is known and thought and what is generally accepted. Realism is not the first word that, with best meaning, has incurred the worst.

Note on Socialist Realism

In the interests of intelligibility I have tried to make this short study loosely progressive, starting with a simple exclusive idea of realism and ending with a more complex inclusive one. In doing so I have probably not avoided the danger of falsification – the history of ideas is never so orderly. It is true, for example, that there is a renewed advocacy at the present time for the kind of deferential contract with reality which I would see as necessarily simplistic – possibly under the influence of phenomenalism, in its attempt to counteract what Ihab Hassan has called 'the source of the mind's alienation, the Cartesian madness of the West' (*Comparative Literature Studies*, I (1964), p. 268). In poetry one might point to the work of William Carlos Williams, fulfilling his dictum 'no ideas but in things', and Gary Snyder with his poems of passive notation; in the novel to the *nouveau roman* of Alain Robbe-Grillet, where metaphor is outlawed and things gather once more to oppress the imagination. Following up in criticism there are books like J. Hillis Miller's *Poets of Reality* (1966) with its contention that 'the mind must efface itself before reality' (p. 7), C. K. Weatherhead's *The Edge of the Image* (Seattle, 1968), advocating the new literalism of William Carlos Williams and Marianne Moore in reaction against the arrogant transformations of the symbolists, and Denis Donoghue's *The Ordinary Universe* (London, 1968), offering to restore 'the proper plenitude of fact' in literature. The interested reader could easily adjust any imbalance in my argument by consulting these works: all of them creating or encouraging a situation where 'art dies back to life' (the phrase is D. J. Enright's, from his poem 'The Old Man Comes to his Senses').

More important, I could not in my main argument conveniently include one significant modern development; that of socialist realism, the realism of Marxist orthodoxy. If naturalism was a rigidification of realism, then socialist realism is a rigidification of what is retrospectively called the 'critical realism' of certain nineteenth-century novelists, particularly Tolstoy. By 'critical realism' (the term is again imported from philosophy) is meant a depiction of contemporary reality which is not aloof and neutral, like Flaubert's, but informed by some moral belief. Ernest J. Simmons has significantly described Tolstoy as 'the conscience of Russia', 'the conscience of the world', 'the conscience of humanity' (in *Leo Tolstoy*, Boston, 1946; cit. Wimsatt and Brooks, *Literary Criticism*, p. 462), and the propounders of this new austere realism have used Tolstoy as the early realists used Balzac and Stendhal to lend authority to their ideas. The authority is readily derived from Tolstoy's very deliberate late document *What Is Art?*, with its uncompromising rejection of most of what passes for art (including Shakespeare and Beethoven) as corrupt, and its insistence on the simple art of simple feelings which must take its place and help to bring about the brotherhood of man. Tolstoy's emphasis was moral, religious (not unlike George Eliot's); but the emphasis in socialist realism is wholly political. Georg Lukács in *The Meaning of Contemporary Realism* (1957; trans. 1962) makes it clear that socialist realism is founded on a rigorous distinction between the falsification of subjectivity and the rectification of the subjective-objective dialectic:

> We arrive, therefore, at an important distinction: the modernist writer identifies what is necessarily a subjective experience with reality as such, thus giving a distorted picture of reality as a whole (Virginia Woolf is an extreme example of this). The realist, with his critical detachment, places what is a significant, specifically modern experience in a wider context, giving it only the emphasis it deserves as part of a greater objective whole.

Virginia Woolf is singled out here, but Joyce and especially Kafka are Lukács's typical exemplars of the 'attenuation of actuality' in modernist writing (p. 25). Against their 'static and sensational' he sets Thomas Mann's 'dynamic and developmental' view of the world (p. 19).

So long as socialist realism proposes a genuine synthesis of subjective and objective it answers the ideals examined in the third chapter: there could even be an improbable parallel drawn with surrealism itself – peculiarly offensive to the socialist realist – which believes in 'the future reconciliation of these two states, dream and reality, apparently so contradictory, in a sort of absolute reality' (Breton, *Manifestes du Surréalisme*, p. 27). But with socialist realism the synthesis is illusory, or at least artificial, because the 'absolute reality' which shall be discovered by the process of dialectic is pre-determined; it must be a socialist reality, conforming to a political ideal. 'Absence of meaning', says Lukács, 'reduces art to naturalistic description' (p. 36); the meaning which informs the description must be the vision of a socialist society. A. A. Zhdanov declared at the first All Soviet Congress of Writers in 1934 that the writer must depict life 'not simply as "objective reality," but ... in its revolutionary development'; Maxim Gorky had earlier allowed that 'revolutionary romanticism' was another possible name for socialist realism, 'the purpose of which is not only to depict the past critically, but chiefly to promote the consolidation of revolutionary achievement in the present and a clearer view of the lofty objectives of the socialist future' (in *DMLR*, p. 487). And so for Lukács 'a correct aesthetic understanding of social and historical reality is the precondition of realism'; although eventually this precondition will be unnecessary, since 'society will eventually achieve a condition which only socialist realism can adequately describe' (pp. 97, 115). Socialist realism is true 'by definition' (p. 100); we have relapsed into the most baffling circular dogmatism. Socialist realism reassumes the austere attitude approved by Plato in his *Republic*, rationalized as part of a modern political theory and enforced by an authority which believes this to be unchallengeable. Lukács rejects the synonym 'revolutionary romanticism', but the phrase of Gorky's is a useful reminder that far from being dispassionately or even critically objective, socialist realism is in fact intensely idealist in its assumptions.

So the term when properly understood is self-disqualifying. Lukács claims that 'in no other aesthetic does the truthful depiction of reality have so central a place as in Marxism' (p. 101), but this is simple tautology because the attribution of truth is reserved for Marxist reality. Socialist realism, then, discovers a new distortion for the word realism, distinct from both the conscientious realism and the conscious realism of my own analysis.

Bibliography

The literature of realism is very extensive, especially in French, both in source material and critical commentary; the following list pretends to include only a brief selection, chosen for their importance, usefulness, or availability. There is a fuller bibliography in Becker's work (listed below), though this is neither exhaustive nor always reliable.

PRIMARY SOURCES

I have not troubled to specify an edition of texts which are generally available, but have simply given the date of first publication.

BALZAC, HONORÉ DE, 'Avant-Propos' to *La Comédie Humaine*, 1842.

BAUDELAIRE, CHARLES, *Oeuvres Complètes*, Paris, 1954.

BRETON, ANDRÉ, *Manifestes du Surréalisme*, ed. J.-J. Pauvert, 1962.

CHAMPFLEURY, *Le Réalisme*, Paris, 1857.

DESNOYERS, FERNAND, 'Du Réalisme' in *L'Artiste*, 9 December 1855, pp. 197–200.

DURANTY, EDMOND, *Réalisme*, Paris, July 1856–May 1857.

FLAUBERT, GUSTAVE, *Correspondance*, Paris, 1926–33.

GAUTIER, THÉOPHILE, *Mademoiselle de Maupin*, 1835.

GONCOURT, JULES & EDMOND DE, *Germinie Lacerteux*, 1864.

GONCOURT, JULES, *Les Frères Zemganno*, 1879.

HUYSMANS, J.-K., *Là-Bas*, 1891.

JAMES, HENRY, *Notes on Novelists*, New York, 1916.

JAMES, HENRY, *The Art of the Novel*, New York, 1934.

MAUPASSANT, GUY DE, *Pierre et Jean*, 1888.

TAINE, HIPPOLYTE, *Histoire de la Littérature Anglaise*, Paris, 1863–4.

TAINE, HIPPOLYTE, *Nouveaux Essais de Critiqu eet d'Histoire*, Paris, 1865.

TOLSTOY, LEO, *What is Art?* 1898; trans. Aylmer Maude, London, 1930.

WILDE, OSCAR, *The Decay of Lying*, 1889.

ZOLA, ÉMILE, *Mes Haines*, 1866.

ZOLA, ÉMILE, *Thérèse Raquin*, 1868.

ZOLA, ÉMILE, *Le Roman Expérimental*, 1880.

ZOLA, ÉMILE, *Les Romanciers Naturalistes*, 1881.

SECONDARY SOURCES

AUERBACH, ERICH, *Mimesis*, 1946; trans. Willard Trask, Princeton, 1953.
Classic study sees realism achieved by breakdown of conventions, from Homer onwards, and fully achieved in nineteenth-century France.

BECKER, GEORGE J., *Documents of Modern Literary Realism*, Princeton, 1963.
600 pp. anthology from many languages with useful introduction and bibliography: a good starting-point for research.

BECKETT, SAMUEL, *Proust*, London, 1931.
Long essay involves a refined repudiation of the realist-naturalist aesthetic.

BOOTH, WAYNE C., *The Rhetoric of Fiction*, Chicago, 1961.
Full study of theory of the novel deals with realism in ch. 2 and passim. See also bibliography (part II c) and references in index

BORNECQUE, J.-H. & COGNY, P., *Réalisme et Naturalisme*, Paris, 1958.
Excellent short study broken down under intelligible headings. Liberal quotation from primary sources.

CROUZET, MARCEL, *Duranty*, Paris, 1964.
An extensive study whose ample footnotes provide minute documentation of realism 'as it happened' in France.

DONOGHUE, DENIS, *The Ordinary Universe*, London, 1968.
Argues on behalf of the 'proper plenitude of fact' in literature.

GRAHAM, KENNETH, *English Criticism of the Novel 1865–1900*, Oxford, 1965.
Ch. 2 provides documentation of the English response to the realist experiment.

HONAN, PARK (ed.), 'Realism, Reality, and the Novel.' A Symposium in *Novel* II, 1969, pp. 197–211.
Conversation between Frank Kermode and others brings the discussion up to date.

LACHER, WALTER, *Le Réalisme dans le roman contemporain*, Geneva, 1940.
Extends the meaning of realism to accommodate twentieth-century novelists.

LEVIN, HARRY, 'What is Realism?' in *Comparative Literature*, III, 1951, pp. 193–9.
Introduces an issue on realism by posing the basic questions.

LEVIN, HARRY, *The Gates of Horn*, New York, 1963.
Study of Stendhal, Balzac, Flaubert, Zola, Proust against a broad background of novel theory.

LUKÁCS, GEORG, *The Meaning of Contemporary Realism*, 1958; trans. J. and N. Mander, London, 1962.
Apologia for socialist realism.

MARTINO, PIERRE, *Le Roman realiste sous le second empire*, Paris, 1913.

MARTINO, PIERRE, *Le Naturalisme Français*, Paris, 1923.
Compact studies of theory and practice in these successive movements.

MCDOWALL, ARTHUR, *Realism: A Study in Art and Thought*, London, 1918.
Critical rather than historical account that achieves a very satisfying perspective.

MILLER, J. HILLIS, *Poets of Reality*, Cambridge, Mass., 1965.
Important qualification of symbolist theory.

ORTEGA Y GASSET, JOSE, *The Dehumanization of Art and Notes on the Novel*, trans. Helene Weyl, Princeton, 1948.
Two brilliant, suggestive essays.

PASSMORE, JOHN, *A Hundred Years of Philosophy*, London, 1957; Penguin ed., Harmondsworth, 1968.
An excellent account of Realism, Critical Realism, and New Realism in Philosophy since 1850.

SCHOLES, ROBERT, *The Fabulators*, New York, 1967.
Builds new theory on the ruins of realism: dedicated to expose 'the artificiality of the real and the reality of the artificial'.

STEVENS, WALLACE, *Opus Posthumous*, New York, 1957
Poet's forays into the no-man's-land between reality and imagination.

STROMBERG, R. S., *Realism, Naturalism, and Symbolism*, New York, 1968.
Some make-weight extracts from novels, etc., but other passages provide useful intellectual background to the period.

SYMONS, ARTHUR, *The Symbolist Movement in Literature*, London, 1899.
Pioneering study of the symbolists; still very readable.

TERTZ, ABRAM [pseudonym of Andrei Sinyavsky], *On Socialist Realism*, New York, 1960.
Critique of socialist realism from the inside.

VOGÜÉ, ÉMILE DE, *Le Roman Russe*, Paris, 1886.
'Avant-Propos' (translated in *DMLR*) the best short introduction to the nineteenth-century context of realism.

WEATHERHEAD, C. K., *The Edge of the Image*, Seattle, 1968.
Argument for a return to literalism in poetry.

WELLEK, RENÉ, 'The Concept of Realism in Literary Scholarship' in *Concepts of Criticism*, New Haven, 1963, pp. 222–55.

WILLIAMS, RAYMOND, *The Long Revolution*, London, 1961.
Chs. 1 and 7 offer redefinitions of creativity and realism.

WIMSATT, W. K. & BROOKS, CLEANTH, *Literary Criticism*, London, 1957.
Ch. 21 deals dismissively with realist aesthetics.

Addition to Second Edition:

JOSIPOVICI, GABRIEL, *The World and the Book*, London, 1971.
An eclectic exploration of the relationship between the writer's world and his medium.

Index